THE DAR[K SIDE] OF T[HE MOON]

by Don Nigro

A Play in Two Acts

S A M U E L   F R E N C H ,   I N C .

45 WEST 25TH STREET   NEW YORK 10010

7623 SUNSET BOULEVARD   HOLLYWOOD 90046

LONDON   *TORONTO*

IMPORTANT BILLING AND CREDIT
REQUIREMENTS

All producers of THE DARK SONNETS OF THE LADY must give credit to the Author of the Play in all programs distributed in connection with performances of the Play and in all instances in which the title of the Play appears for purposes of advertising, publicizing or otherwise exploiting the Play and/or a production. The name of the Author *must* also appear on a separate line, on which no other name appears, immediately following the title, and *must* appear in size of type not less than fifty percent the size of the title type.

The Dark Sonnets of the Lady was first produced by the OSU Department of Theatre, Firman H. Brown, Chairman, in the Stadium II Theatre at the Ohio State University in Columbus, Ohio in April of 1985 with the following cast:

Dora .... Amy L. Eddings
Mother .... Leah Hocking
Father .... Jefferson Cronin
Wolf..................................... Thomas Rice
Marcy .... Angela Barch
Herr Klippstein .... Robert Moore
Frau Klippstein ....Patricia Fochtman
Freud.................................. Van Ackerman

Directed by Don Nigro
Scenic Coordination by William J. Winsor
Costume Design by Pamela Keech
Lighting Design by M.E. Kirk
Sound Design by Steve Nelson
Choreography by Robin Pyle
Dramaturgy by Vicki A. Sanders
Technical Direction by Joseph Walter
Stage Manager: Gretchen Furlow
Assistant Stage Manager: Jennifer Flint

The play was subsequently produced at the McCarter Theatre in Princeton, New Jersey, Nagle Jackson, Artistic Director, in March of 1988 with the following cast:

Dora	Kate Fuglei
Mother	Peggy Cowles
Father	Ian Stuart
Wolf	Mark Brown
Marcy	Leslie Brett Daniels
Herr Klippstein	Richard Leighton
Frau Klippstein	Elizabeth Hess
Freud	Richard Council

Directed by Robert Lanchester
Set Design by John Jensen
Costume Design by Gregg Barnes
Lighting Design by Victor En Yu Tan
Sound Design by Stephen Smith
Choreography by Nancy Thiel
Stage Manager: Peter C.Cook
Assistant Stage Manager: Megan Miller-Shields
Literary Manager: Sandra Moscovitz

This production was made possible by grants from the New Jersey State Council on the Arts/Department of State and the Geraldine R. Dodge Foundation.

The Dark Sonnets of the Lady was a finalist play for the National Repertory Theatre Foundation's National Play Award.

CHARACTERS

Freud, mid-forties
Father, forties
Mother, forties
Dora, eighteen
Wolf, twenties
Herr Klippstein, late thirties
Frau Klippstein, thirty
Marcy, twenty

SETTING

Vienna in the fall and early winter of the year 1900, and other times and places, 1896 to 1902. The unit set is all locations simultaneously, including Freud's desk, chair and couch, a sofa and other versatile pieces of furniture for Dora's house, the dining room at the hotel, an upstage bed, the sitting room at the lake, Herr Klippstein's office, a street, the lake shore, the dock, stairs leading to various levels. Each part of the stage will become various locations in the course of the play. Downstage there is a window seat above which a largely or entirely imaginary frame becomes in turn a window, a mirror, a picture frame, depending on how the characters relate to it at any given moment. What any part of the stage represents at any given time depends on what the characters are doing there. The people are the real geography. The unit set is essential: there must be no set changes, except for the natural migration of props and sometimes wooden chairs around the set in the course of the play, moved naturally by the actors in character. Mother is very useful in this respect, as her obsession with cleaning allows her to move with great freedom while her scenes or other scenes are playing to remove props, relocate chairs, whatever is necessary. Marcy may also be helpful here, and it is also her main responsibility to care for the two Klippstein children, Peter and Grindl, who are life-size rag dolls dressed in Victorian children's clothing, with no hair or facial features and buttons for eyes. If props or children need rearrangement between acts, Marcy or Mother should come out during the intermission waltzes and do so in character. Time and space are fluid and except for a few brief costume changes all the characters should be visible and animate on the set throughout the play. When not directly involved in scenes, the characters watch or perform other related actions from other parts of the set, and should usually well before the end of one scene be already in place for the next—ease of transition being absolutely essential to the flow of the play. Dora may look at Freud from across the stage and cut into or out of any scene whenever necessary and be instantly in another. Time and space constantly interpenetrate. Absolutely no blackouts except where specifically indicated. Each scene flows directly into the next with no breaks and no dead spaces. The numbering of scenes is for the convenience of the director and the actors only—the action is always continuous. Under no circumstances should accents of any kind be superimposed upon the text.

ACT I

Scene 1

We have been listening for some time to Strauss WALTZES, and towards the end of this last one, the "Emperor", LIGHTS have begun to come down on the house and up slowly on the shadowy set. Now, at the sound of the horn that announces the last section of the waltz, DORA appears, moves to the center, makes as if to dance, shyly, to the violin introduction to the return of the main waltz theme, but stops as her eyes meet those of MOTHER, who has come into the parlor to dust as the main theme begins. FATHER enters a few bars later as the main theme repeats, moves to Freud's office, looks out the window. WOLF enters on the little violin phrase at the end of Father's section, moves to his chair, sits. MARCY appears in the lovely, lush section that follows, pushing the baby carriage containing the two DOLL CHILDREN, wheeling them around the edge of the set. HERR KLIPPSTEIN strolls in on the stronger section of horns that follows, and then FRAU KLIPPSTEIN on the gentle flute section that is next, meeting Dora's eyes briefly. Then as the final, military section swells, FREUD enters, gets a cigar from the box on his desk, and seats himself at his desk as the waltz climaxes and ends. The PEOPLE freeze momentarily in the brief silence that follows and there is a click and shutter effect of the LIGHTS—a photograph of the group, the essence of which is a sense of isolation, each person from the others. Then immediately FREUD begins, in mid-consultation with FATHER, as the OTHERS go calmly about their business, MOTHER dusting, MARCY taking care of the children, et cetera.

FREUD. I presume you acquired this infection before your marriage.

FATHER. Of course I did. What kind of man do you think I am?

FREUD. I have no idea, but if I'm going to help you, I need to ask questions, and I expect the truth.

FATHER. I understand that. Is this thing fixable?

FREUD. I can treat it.

FATHER. My sister told me you're a very gifted man. You treated her once for a nervous disorder, I think.

FREUD. Yes, I remember. How is she?

FATHER. Oh, she's all right. Well, actually, she's dead. Not your fault. I think you also treated my brother Otto. Old crazy Otto, we used to call him.

(FREUD looks at him.)

FATHER. Affectionately, we called him that.

FREUD. A very unfortunate man.

FATHER. Oh, I don't know. He seems happy as a lark. He imitates farm animals. He's quite good, if you like that sort of thing. Look, tell me the truth, are nervous illnesses like that sometimes—uh—passed around in a family?

FREUD. That's possible. Why do you ask?

FATHER. Oh, not for me—I'm normal enough. I think I am. It's my daughter I'm worried about.

MOTHER. Dora, why don't you ever help me with the cleaning?

FATHER. My daughter is a remarkable girl. Lovely, intelligent—I can't describe how dear she is to me, to all of us.

DORA. Mother, Daddy is going to get well, isn't he?

MOTHER. Is your father sick again? What an unhealthy man he is. You'd better stay away from him. I wish I had. No telling what you'll catch. Dust around the china bull there, dear, that's a good girl. No, THERE.

FATHER. We're very close. At least, we HAVE been close.

DORA. I don't know what I'd do if something happened to Daddy.

FATHER. (*Speaking across the stage to Dora.*) My Dora is a wonderful little charmer. She'll do fine no matter what happens to her poor old Daddy.

DORA. But I don't like you being sick all the time, it's very selfish of you.

FATHER. Then I'll go up to Vienna and visit Dr. Freud and he'll fix me up, all right?

DORA. Is Dr. Freud a good man?

FATHER. Your Aunt Sylvie and Uncle Otto said he's the best.

DORA. But Aunt Sylvie's dead, and Uncle Otto's a lunatic.

MOTHER. Oh, I like Otto. Last time I saw him he was mooing like a cow. A little disconcerting for the dinner guests, I will admit, him talking to his food, leering at the roast beef, giggling at the cream—but I got used to it.

(*Looking at Father.*) Amazing what one can get used to. Get that spot over by the foot warmer, dear.

FATHER. (*To Freud.*) I wonder if you'd consent to see Dora, just to reassure us that nothing is seriously wrong with her. It would make us all feel a bit more at ease.

FREUD. What exactly is your daughter's problem?

FATHER. She faints, has headaches, shortness of breath, abdominal pains, but the doctors can't find a physical cause for any of it. She's been enormously depressed, and her mother just found something she wrote which alarms us very much.

DORA. "Dear Mama and Papa. I've been thinking much recently about death, and how peaceful it must be, and how clean."

MOTHER. Dora, why don't you polish the silverware?

FATHER. (*Passing the table where the KLIPPSTEINS are having tea with MARCY and the CHILDREN.*) And she's been imagining things, outrageous things about me, about our friends the Klippsteins, and she's become increasingly rude to her mother, and this I cannot tolerate.

DORA. I polished the silverware Tuesday.

MOTHER. If you don't polish the silverware it rots.

DORA. Silverware doesn't rot, Mother, people rot.

MOTHER. Of course they do, but we don't mind rubbing them once in a while, do we? So polish the silverware like a good girl, and God will maybe smile on you and find you a husband.

DORA. We never use the silverware.

MOTHER. We should use our best silverware to eat with? Put it in our mouths? How do we know what's been in there? What are we, the Archduke? Your hands are dirty, Dora, wash your hands.

DORA. My hands are clean.

MOTHER. Dirty hands, dirty mind.

DORA. My hands are red from so much washing.

MOTHER. Such a beautiful girl you are, Dora, such sad eyes, such a delicate figure, so graceful, so smart, such lovely hair, and no man in his right mind will look at you, do you know why?

DORA. Because I'm smarter than they are.

MOTHER. Because look at your hands, they look like crab meat, disgusting, and so dirty, and also you're much too skinny. Are you sick?

DORA. No, Mother, I'm fine.

MOTHER. You look sick.

DORA. I'm fine.

MOTHER. You don't look well at all.

DORA. I'm sorry, Mother.

MOTHER. In fact, you look awful.

DORA. I'm doing the best I can.

MOTHER. You look like something the cat threw up. Do you know what Frau Klippstein says?

FRAU K. She doesn't care what I say.

MOTHER. She says your father is right, you should go see that nice doctor, what's his name?

DORA. I don't need a doctor. I hate doctors. I can't breathe.

MOTHER. You don't want to be a potato head like your Uncle Otto, do you?

DORA. I'm all right, I just can't breathe.

MOTHER. I think his name is Fudd. Yes, Siegfried Fudd.

DORA. It's Freud, Mother, Sigmund Freud, and I'm NOT going to see him.

(FREUD stands, holds out bne hand to her from his office. SHE looks across the stage at him, very suspicious.)

Scene 2

FREUD. Hello, Dora. How are you today?

DORA. Is that a trick question?

FREUD. You don't trust me very much, do you?

DORA. I don't trust you at all. Is that necessary?

FREUD. It would help. Why don't you come over and sit down?

DORA. I don't like offices. They have ulterior motives.

FREUD. You mean people in offices have ulterior motives.

DORA. No, I mean offices. You walk in and they begin to eat you and digest you and after a while you disappear.

FREUD. Do you believe that?

DORA. Of course I do. I'm totally insane. Isn't that what my father told you?

FREUD. He told me you're unhappy and asked me to try and help you.

DORA. How much is he paying you?

FREUD. Enough.

DORA. Just to talk to me?

FREUD. More or less.

DORA. Some job.

FREUD. I like it.

DORA. All right, we might as well get it over with, ask me your stupid doctor questions. Come on, earn your money.

FREUD. What kind of questions would you like?

DORA. Well, I don't want to tell you your business, but it's customary, after the usual vacuous and patronizing introductory remarks, to ask if I had any serious illnesses as a child.

FREUD. Did you have any serious illnesses as a child?

DORA. Hundreds. Chicken pox, mumps, beriberi, leprosy—my brother Wolf got everything first, very mild cases, then he'd give them to ME and I'd be flat on my back forever. Hateful position, that. I don't recommend it.

FREUD. Do you blame your brother for this?

DORA. Yes, I think he did it on purpose.

FREUD. Do you love your brother?

DORA. I liked him better before he started acting like an adult.

FREUD. You don't want to be an adult?

DORA. Not that kind.

FREUD. What kind?

(WOLF is moving across to the sofa with his paper as MOTHER dusts.)

MOTHER. Wolf, if you walk on my clean floor with your dirty feet, you are not my son.

DORA. Where do you want him to walk? On the furniture?

MOTHER. Dora, you're such a funny little person. Sit down and sew me some doilies.

DORA. We have thousands of doilies, don't we, Wolf?

WOLF. (*Reading his paper.*) Hmmmmmmm?

MOTHER. A woman can never have too many doilies. And don't sit there, Dora, you'll mess the cover your Uncle

Otto made at the rest home. Shame on you, what a worthless girl you are.

DORA. Wolf, tell Mother to stop picking on me.

MOTHER. Yes, Wolf, here, go on, cut off these fingers that wiped your little bottoms on many a day after you grunted in your pants, and not so long ago, either. You know, we missed a spot there when we waxed the floor.

DORA. Sometimes I wish I was with Uncle Otto.

WOLF. You're too sensitive, Dora. Mother means well.

MOTHER. How do you know what I mean?

DORA. You used to take my side, Wolf, when we were small. We used to take baths together. Now you never do.

WOLF. You want to take baths together?

MOTHER. Wolf is a grown up boy, now, Dora, he doesn't want to take baths with his sister, he's got better people to take baths with.

WOLF. (*Looking at Marcy.*) I wish.

MOTHER. What's that?

WOLF. I said I want fish. For supper.

MOTHER. (*Fussing with his hair.*) Anything you want, but not tonight. You should grow up, too, Dora, like your brother. Such a grown up little Wolfie, yes. You have fleas, did you know that?

DORA. I think my only friend in this house is my father, and lately I've begun to wonder about him, too.

MOTHER Yes, go on, kill your mother with words like butcher knives. Maybe we've got lamb for supper.

WOLF. It's all right, Mother. Dora's not herself. She hasn't been herself for some time.

DORA. Yes, Dora's somebody else entirely. Dora's an imposter.

MOTHER. I think so, too. I don't think you're my daughter at all. Sometimes, Wolf, I think your sister, God forgive me, is illegitimate.

WOLF. Mother—

MOTHER. Yes, I think she's your father's child, but not mine.

WOLF. How could that be? You gave birth to her, didn't you?

DORA. How's Mother supposed to remember back that far? She can't even remember what she had for breakfast.

MOTHER. Dora, why don't you go bother Frau Klippstein for a while? Or go find your father. Where is he? And what DID we have for breakfast?

DORA. I don't feel good. I can't breathe.

MOTHER. Maybe we forgot breakfast, and that's why I can't remember and you feel sick. Frau Klippstein says—

DORA. Mother, will you please be quiet a minute? I can't breathe.

MOTHER. If you're waiting for me to come and fuss over you, Dora, don't hold your breath.

DORA. DADDY.

FREUD. You often can't breathe?

DORA. I sometimes can't breathe. They make me so angry. Wolf's grown more like Mother as I've grown like Father.

FREUD. How are you like your father?

DORA. I'm smart, and stubborn. But I tell the truth.

FREUD. And your father lies?

DORA. Only when it's convenient.

FREUD. What does he lie about?

DORA. I'm sure he's lied to you about me.

FREUD. He said you have severe headaches and other symptoms for no apparent reason. You cough, lose your voice, and can't breathe.

(DORA coughs. FREUD writes something down.)

DORA. What did you write?

FREUD. A note to myself.

DORA. What kind of note?

FREUD. It would mean little to you.

DORA. Are you going to be one of those stupid mysterious doctors? I'd hoped for better from you. Uncle Otto spoke so highly of you one day when he was in the garden trumpeting like an elephant.

FREUD. I take it you've been to many doctors.

DORA. Oh, I'm the toast of Vienna. Are you jealous?

FREUD. Certainly.

DORA. Father adores doctors. He calls one every time his bowels move. Our house is like a French farce, with doctors running madly in and out. I hate old men poking and leering and making friendly remarks about the weather while fingering my privates. From a woman's point of view, doctors are a kind of torture chamber. Present company excepted, at least for the present.

FREUD. I'm not presently a torture chamber?

DORA. You're not much of anything yet. At least you're relatively well behaved. So far.

FREUD. I only poke at your mind.

DORA. Vicarious molestation.

(FREUD writes something, smiling.)

DORA. What are you writing now?

FREUD. Suppose we make a deal. I promise to tell you exactly what I'm thinking, whenever you ask, as honestly as I can, if you promise me the same.

DORA. Including what you write down?

FREUD. Including what I write down.

DORA. All right. What did you write?

(HE hands her the pad. SHE reads:)

DORA. "This is one smart cookie." Is that what I am, clinically speaking? As opposed to, say, three dumb cookies or one smart cupcake? Am I supposed to be flattered?

FREUD. I don't care. It's good that you're smart, but it's also potentially a danger.

DORA. I know. They hate you if you're smart.

FREUD. Who does?

DORA. Everyone.

FREUD. Does everyone hate you?

DORA. *(Looking out the window at MOTHER, who is cleaning it from the other side.)* They would if I didn't make a point of acting as stupid as possible every now and then, in self-defense. *(Turning back to Freud.)* I'll bet everybody hates YOU.

FREUD. The danger I mean is that the smarter the patient, the more elaborate the defense they build to keep me from finding what I need to know.

DORA. Is this going to be a war then?

FREUD. Maybe a small war. Between friends. To help you.

DORA. And not you?

FREUD. Maybe to help me a little, too.

DORA. Do you think because Aunt Sylvie was a bit looney and Uncle Otto makes animal noises that I'm in some degree looney also?

FREUD. I don't use words like that.

DORA. You also treated Father. Is he looney too?

FREUD. Your father had an infection.

DORA. What kind of infection?

FREUD. I'm afraid professional ethics—

DORA. No, I don't think he was infected by professional ethics, I think Father's immune to that. You're breaking our agreement.

FREUD. Your father had a social infection which many men contract.

DORA. Is this dirty, or what?

FREUD. It's a part of life.

DORA. I'm sure it is. My father and his family are all intelligent, creative people—they lie, become lunatics, and contract unspeakable diseases. Mother and her family are much more respectable—they're all morons. If I prove too interesting I'll be judged insane or a liar, is that about it?

FREUD. I don't judge, I ask questions and I pay attention. This is an investigation into truth you and I are making together. We're explorers in a dark, unknown place, and no one can tell what we'll find.

DORA. That's very impressive of us. Does it make you uncomfortable that your fellow explorer is a woman? This is virgin territory, you know.

(MOTHER, who has been dusting and poking about in the window seat, finds a note and begins reading it laboriously.)

MOTHER. "Dear Mama and Papa—"

FREUD. I find women fascinating fellow explorers, although often puzzling and sometimes treacherous.

DORA. Yes, I'm very treacherous, but I'm disappointed that I puzzle you. I thought you were going to have all the answers at your fingertips, Doctor. You make me lose confidence in you, and then I get bored and have to go. Are we about done?

FREUD. Why did you write the suicide note?

MOTHER. (*Having read to the end, screaming.*) AAHHHHHHHH. OH, NOOOO. DOOORA. MY LITTLE DORRY. OH, GOD, HEINRICH, HEINRICH—

DORA. Because I love watching Mother have hysterics.

FREUD. Why did you want to die?

DORA. I didn't want to die, I never meant anyone to see it. She's always poking around in my private things, she cleans all day, she must polish my father in bed at night. I think a woman who messes about with another woman's property should be killed.

FREUD. If you didn't want them to see it, why did you write it?

DORA. For my own amusement.

FREUD. Threatening suicide amuses you?

DORA. Writing amuses me.

FREUD. You never intended to harm yourself?

DORA. I intended to see what I'd write, a kind of investigation into truth, as it were—and look where my creative and exploratory impulses got me—here with you. My parents panicked, that's their standard mode of operation.

FREUD. Do you ever feel you want to die?

DORA. At the moment I'd consider it. I don't like this conversation. In fact, I feel a bit faint.

FREUD. That's convenient.

DORA. I beg your pardon?

FREUD. Do you often have fainting spells in the middle of conversations you don't like?

DORA. I'm sure Father's told you all about it.

FREUD. Do you faint when you argue with your father?

DORA. I don't argue with my father.

FREUD. Even about the Klippsteins?

DORA. What did he tell you about the Klippsteins? Did he say I've been imagining things? I've got a great imagination, I get it from my father. No doubt he denied everything.

FREUD. Denied what?

DORA. You won't believe me.

FREUD. Try me and see.

DORA. My father's been having an affair with Frau Klippstein.

FREUD. How do you know that?

DORA. It isn't hard to figure out. They're about as discreet as the Russian army. I run into them on the street with great regularity, pawing at each other and giggling like hyenas.

(FATHER and FRAU KLIPPSTEIN are walking together in the street and laughing. To them—)

Scene 3

DORA. Could you direct me to the zoo? It's mating season, Uncle Otto's so excited.

FRAU K. Hello, Dora.

DORA. Don't let me interrupt your party.

FATHER. (*To Frau Klippstein.*) So be sure and tell your husband what I said, and he and I will discuss it later over cigars, all right?

DORA. Sounds swell to me.

FATHER. Dora, why are you here?

DORA. I was just going to ask you that.

FATHER. I had an appointment, and on the way I ran into Frau Klippstein and remembered I had a message for her husband.

DORA. What kind of message?

FATHER. Nothing that concerns you.

FRAU K. It's just about those awful chess games they play. They're getting together tomorrow. What a thing for grown men to do, playing games.

FATHER. I find it relaxing.

DORA. You look relaxed.

FATHER. I'm sure you two have a lot to chatter about, so I'll just hop along to my appointment.

DORA. Yes, you just hop along. Hop, hop.

FATHER. I'll see you later, Dora.

DORA. I can hardly wait.

(HE goes. DORA and FRAU K look at each other.)

FRAU K. So how are you today?

DORA. What do you and my father do all the time?

FRAU K. Do? What do we do?

DORA. Why do I always see you in the street with him?

FRAU K. Your father's a good friend of my husband, you know that. Our families have been close for years, and I don't see—

DORA. But what do you want with him? You've got a husband. And what does he want with you?

FRAU K. I don't think your father owes you any explanations, Dora, and I don't like the tone of that.

DORA. I used to think you were such a good person.

FRAU K. And now you don't? Dora, just what awful things do you think I've done?

DORA. What if I tell Mother? It would kill her.

FRAU K. Your mother wouldn't have the slightest idea what you were talking about. I scarcely know myself. Don't look so glum. You and I have always been such good friends. You're the best friend I have in the world, you mustn't think bad things about me. I'm quite innocent, I swear. And more important, you mustn't distress your father, who is, given the unreliability of men in general, probably the finest one you'll ever know.

DORA. Finer than your husband?

FRAU K. (*Looking at Herr K.*) There's room enough for two fine men in the world. Don't read filth into everything you see, Dora, it's really not a very pleasant way to live, being jealous and suspicious all the time. Look, let's play at being adults and stop for tea. We can have a nice talk and giggle together like the old days. Dora, please?

DORA. I hate tea, it tastes like boiled vomit.

FRAU K. All right, if you insist on being unpleasant, I'll let you alone. If you don't like me any more, you don't like me any more. Maybe you'll like me again tomorrow. Poor Dora, so unhappy over nothing. (*SHE kisses Dora on the forehead.*) Well, I love you, so there, no matter what horrible things you make up about me. I'm going off to buy myself a ridiculous hat, you've depressed me so much. Come along if you like. No? Try to be happy, darling, your whole life's ahead of you, don't waste time worrying about us. Find yourself a nice young man and be happy. Your life is a tiny flame in an enormous dark room, it's such a frail thing, so brief and uncertain. You've got to find a way to get through it with some sort of joy. I'll come and see you tomorrow, all right?

(DORA looks away. FRAU KLIPPSTEIN sighs and goes. DORA starts to call her back, then resists the urge.)

Scene 4

FREUD. (*Watching Frau K walk away.*) Should a woman who messes about with another woman's husband also be killed? What about another woman's father? Or another woman's lover?

DORA. Just the men should be killed.

FREUD. That hardly seems fair.

DORA. I think it's fair. You make women weak, conniving, selfish, lust-crazed, and then you persecute them for it. I think men should be castrated at birth, solve all the world's problems.

FREUD. I take it you didn't accept Frau Klippstein's explanation.

DORA. Would you have?

FREUD. Did your father speak to you about this later?

DORA. Oh, yes.

FATHER. I merely ran into her in the street.

DORA. And did you also run into her in private? How many times altogether did you run into her, and with what velocity?

FATHER. Dora, don't be smart.

DORA. No, we can't have me being smart! Be nice and stupid like a lady, Dora. Be blind, also, and maybe deaf.

FATHER. It was perfectly innocent.

DORA. You touched her back. You kissed her. I saw you.

FATHER. It was merely a friendly gesture. Your own impure thoughts lead you to imagine the worst in others.

DORA. MY impure thoughts? Anybody in the street could read YOUR impure thoughts. You look at her like a dog looks at hamburger.

FATHER. I will not have you speaking to me this way.

DORA. You sleep with her, don't you? You lie naked in rooms with her in the afternoon and then you come out on the street in your clothes and smile at the world like a monkey. I'm surprised a man your age can manage it.

FATHER. (*Making as if to hit her.*) You are a terrible, wicked girl.

DORA. Yes, hit me, let's see how you really feel about your daughter who gets in the way and isn't stupid enough to believe your pathetic lies.

FATHER. Dora, why do you torture yourself like this? Come here. (*HE moves to embrace her.*)

DORA. Get away, get your hands off me, they smell like her.

FATHER. Dora, listen, Frau Klippstein and I—

DORA. I can't see. Daddy, I can't see. Help me.

FATHER. (*Holding her.*) It's all right.

FREUD. This fainting is of course merely a device to get attention, to end unpleasant scenes with everybody's sympathy, and to get closer to your father, as well as to make him feel guilty and to avoid hearing the truth.

DORA. That is a vile and a very cold lie.

FREUD. You use this fainting to replace Frau Klippstein in your father's arms, you see?

DORA. (*Pulling sharply away from Father.*) That isn't true.

FREUD. Of course it's true. Your anger confirms it. This is the elementary part, anyone can see this, you see it yourself. We must dig much deeper if we're going to find out what the real problem is.

DORA. I don't like you.

FREUD. You'll like me again.

DORA. Who says I ever liked you?

FREUD. You get angry with your father, but then you like him again. The depth of your anger is in part a measure of your love for him. Do you forgive Frau Klippstein as well?

DORA. I hate Frau Klippstein.

FREUD. But you haven't always hated her.

DORA. We used to sometimes do things together.

FREUD. What kind of things?

Scene 5

(FRAU KLIPPSTEIN combing Dora's hair. FATHER and HERR KLIPPSTEIN on the couch, smoking cigars. WOLF and MARCY have taken the CHILDREN to the park and are playing with them. MOTHER dusts. FREUD watches.)

FRAU K. (*As SHE combs.*) You're becoming such a lovely girl, Dora.

DORA. What was I before? An ugly girl?

FRAU K. A lovely child.

DORA. I'll never be beautiful like you.

FRAU K. Nonsense. You're much more beautiful than I am.

DORA. You're the only one who thinks so.

FRAU K. Your father thinks so.

DORA. No he doesn't.

FRAU K. Of course he does. So does my husband.

DORA. You're teasing me.

FRAU K. I wouldn't do that.

DORA. Ouch.

FRAU K. Sorry. Tangles. Everyone loves you, Dora, you're young. Nobody pays much attention to me.

DORA. I pay attention to you. I want to be just like you.

FRAU K. If you're just like me, you'll be a very unhappy girl.

DORA. Are you unhappy? Why would you be unhappy? You have beautiful children, a handsome and charming husband—

FRAU K. You think my husband is handsome and charming?

DORA. Of course I do.

FRAU K. As handsome and charming as your father?

DORA. They're both handsome and charming.

FRAU K. Then you and I are very lucky, aren't we?

DORA. You and Mother are lucky, I'm not.

FRAU K. We're lucky to have YOU.

DORA. Does your husband really think I'm beautiful?

FRAU K. Oh, yes.

DORA. OUCH.

FRAU K. Hold still.

DORA. He said I was beautiful?

FRAU K. He didn't have to. I can tell what my husband is thinking. Unfortunately. Listen, if you sit still and be a good girl, maybe later on you'll get a nice banana, would you like that?

DORA. Yes, very much.

FRAU K. I thought you would.

Scene 6

FREUD. So you no longer like Frau Klippstein, and you think your mother an idiot, your brother very dull and your father a liar. Have you at least reserved your affection for Herr Klippstein, who thinks you're beautiful?

DORA. He's the vilest one of all.

FREUD. And what has Herr Klippstein done to deserve this distinction?

DORA. He attacked me and made an indecent proposition to me. No doubt my father told you I imagined this, too.

FREUD. But you didn't imagine it.

DORA. No.

FREUD. And you told your father?

DORA. Of course I did. And he pretended not to believe me.

FREUD. Why would your father pretend not to believe you?

DORA. Because of Frau Klippstein.

FREUD. I don't understand.

DORA. Father doesn't want to lose her. To break with the Klippsteins is unthinkable for him, so he pretends I'm imagining Herr Klippstein's assault.

FREUD. That's a very serious charge.

DORA. You don't believe me, do you?

FREUD. I didn't say that.

DORA. Well, do you or don't you?

FREUD. Tell me what happened with Herr Klippstein.

DORA. It was at the lake. They have a house there, and Father and I went to visit them.

(SHE is walking with HERR K at the lake. BIRD sounds.)

HERR K. You're such a pretty girl, Dora.

DORA. Yes, I know, but don't worry, I'll get over it.

HERR K. Have you got a boyfriend?

DORA. Don't be silly.

HERR K. I'm seldom silly.

DORA. I think boys my age should be killed.

HERR K. You'd prefer perhaps an older man.

DORA. I'd prefer nobody.

HERR K. The days can be lonely and terrible without someone to love. Also the nights.

DORA. I expect they can be equally lonely and terrible WITH someone to love.

HERR K. Ah, a woman of the world.

DORA. Don't make fun of me.

HERR K. I'd never do that. Would you like a cigarette?

DORA. No thank you.

HERR K. For most people the hope of love is all that keeps them going from one day to the next. One continues to hope for love, somehow, sometime, and one goes on. For people like us, that's all there is.

DORA. That's very sad.

HERR K. You're a wise girl after all, aren't you?

(HE reaches out his hand as if to touch her cheek. For a moment THEY are motionless.)

FREUD. And then what?

DORA. Then he made his indecent proposal.

FREUD. Describe it.

DORA. I'm tired, I think that's all for today.

FREUD. No, not yet.

DORA. I'll say when that's all, I'm paying YOU, you're not paying ME, you'll do what I say and like it.

FREUD. In fact, your father is paying me, not you.

DORA. Thank you for reminding me. You ARE his paid flunky, isn't that right? Your job is to convince me I'm sick.

FREUD. My job is to find the truth and help you.

DORA. Do you believe Herr Klippstein behaved indecently towards me at the lake?

FREUD. I believe you believe it.

DORA. Do you believe my father is having an affair with Frau Klippstein?

FREUD. I believe you believe it. Dora—

DORA. You don't believe anything I've told you.

FREUD. I do not deal in belief, I make investigations into truth—

DORA. Whose truth? Yours or mine? Probably my father's truth, since his truth has money behind it. I expect his will win, that's how the world works, isn't it? Your world, and my father's and Herr Klippstein's. You make the rules, you enforce the rules, you smoke your cigars and the money changes hands and the women change hands and that's truth. So much for our mutual promises, Doctor Fudd. Goodbye.

(SHE runs out of his office. FREUD stands there, troubled, thinking. FATHER has been watching, smoking his cigar. FREUD turns to him.)

Scene 7

FREUD. You don't believe your daughter's story about Herr Klippstein's behavior at the lake?

FATHER. Of course not.

FREUD. Has Dora lied to you before?

FATHER. My daughter is not a liar.

FREUD. She's mistaken, then?

FATHER. She's always been a fanciful girl, very sensitive, with strong feelings and a vivid imagination— although very proper and reserved, of course—I don't want you to get the wrong idea.

FREUD. But how could a quick and perceptive girl like Dora mistake Herr Klippstein's attentions so completely?

FATHER. I think she's suffering from some kind of mental shock that's caused her over-active imagination to invent things she's come to believe are true. That's why I brought her here. Aren't you supposed to be telling ME this?

FREUD. You're sure you don't find some danger in a young girl like Dora being in the frequent and often unsupervised company of Herr Klippstein?

FATHER. I can rely on my daughter.

FREUD. But can you rely on Herr Klippstein?

FATHER. I believe Herr Klippstein incapable of such behavior. A man like that isn't dangerous to Dora—she's still a child, and he still treats her like one.

HERR K. (*Calling through the window to DORA, who is across the stage with MARCY, playing with the CHILDREN.*) Doooooora, can you come out to PLAYYYYYYYyyyyyyyy?

DORA. No.

HERR K. Come on, Dorrydooo, we'll play stickball, foxes and goosie, wolf and sheeps unclothing, blind man in the buff, farmer into Dell? Duck duck?

DORA. I don't want to play with you. You're not a nice man.

HERR K. I'm a lonely man, Dora. Help me.

FREUD. So you think highly of Herr Klippstein's character?

FATHER. I wouldn't go that far. I just don't think he'd do such a thing to Dora. He's a civilized man. Although I do not admire him in all respects.

FREUD. In what respects don't you admire him?

FATHER. I don't like the way he treats his wife.

FREUD. He's unkind to her?

FATHER. He's—not a very good husband.

FREUD. Then it IS possible that—

FATHER. No, it's not.

FREUD. Do you think highly of Frau Klippstein?

FATHER. Yes. She's always been a very good friend. To Dora.

FREUD. And to you?

FATHER. She nursed me in my illness.

FREUD. So you ARE close to her, then?

FATHER. What kind of cross-examination is this? It's Dora you're supposed to worry about, not me.

FREUD. I can only help your daughter if I find the truth.

FATHER. Surely you don't believe her accusations about Frau Klippstein and me?

FREUD. To which accusations do you refer?

FATHER. Are you trying to trap me?

FREUD. I'm trying to help Dora. Is that your only objective here?

FATHER. I don't think I like the sound of that.

FREUD. You may take your business elsewhere if you choose.

FATHER. Perhaps I will.

FREUD. Perhaps you should. (*Pause.*)

FATHER. Look, man to man, I'll tell you. Frau Klippstein is a very fine woman and a very unhappy one. I am—as you know, I get nothing from my wife, my relationship with my wife has been for some years less than nothing. Frau Klippstein is a very warm person. We find comfort from our loneliness now and then in each other's companionship and conversation. Dora is young and doesn't understand this. She sees horrible impropriety where there is in fact only two wretched people who need company and sympathy. I'm not ashamed of my friendship with Frau Klippstein, and I resent any attempt to besmirch her honor or my own, even by my poor misguided daughter, whom I love more than anything in the world. You have a daughter, don't you? I hope your home life is happier than mine. If it isn't, then you can understand my position. And if it is, then you have no right to judge me. Now, is there anything else you'd like to know about my private life?

FREUD. Did you confront Herr Klippstein with your daughter's charges against him?

FATHER. I spoke to him about it, yes.

FREUD. And what did he say?

FATHER. He convinced me that Dora had misinterpreted his intentions.

(HERR KLIPPSTEIN is at the chess board.)

FREUD. And how did he do that?

Scene 8

(HERR KLIPPSTEIN and FATHER play chess and smoke cigars.)

HERR K. You don't really believe I'd compromise myself in such a way with the young daughter of a dear friend of our family like yourself? A girl I think of practically as my own daughter?

FATHER. Dora says you did.

HERR K. I think highly of Dora, you know I do, she's a fine girl, but, my friend, to be frank with you, forgive me, but my wife—you know how dearly my wife loves Dora—my wife has told me on more than one occasion that at this time in her life Dora is rather obsessed with, well, with sexual matters. Which is of course totally understandable at her age, I suppose, I mean, I imagine women think about those things, I don't know, but—

FATHER. Your wife told you this?

HERR K. Ask her if you like. I believe—and I blush to say this to you, but I believe Dora has been reading certain books on the physiology of love which unfortunately had been left at our house at the lake by a previous owner. You may verify this with my wife, if you happen to run into her. I think Dora must have become over-excited by her reading and imagined the scene she described to you.

FATHER. You're saying she made up the whole thing?

HERR K. No, I saw Dora a number of times at the lake, and we were alone quite often, as you may remember, but I assure you my private interviews with her were of the most innocent and proper kind. Not unlike, I imagine, your interviews with my wife, say, on similar occasions.

(Pause. THEY look at each other.)

FATHER. I hope you understand. I love Dora very much, and I will not allow her to be hurt in any way by anyone, for any reason. Do you understand this?

HERR K. Oh, I shouldn't worry too much about it if I was you. It's just a stage girls go through. You're a man of the world, you know how women are.

FATHER. Yes. I do.

HERR K. I know you do. I believe we've got a stalemate here. Has your cigar gone out? Mine's still burning. Want a light?

(THEY look at each other over the chess board, HERR KLIPPSTEIN smiling, FATHER not.)

HERR K. I love this game. It's the only game in the world.

Scene 9

(DORA makes a long cross to FREUD, who sits at his desk, smoking his cigar. HE smiles. SHE frowns and sits down.)

FREUD. I'm happy to see you're no longer angry at me.

DORA. I was bored. I decided to come. I may leave again.

(Pause. FREUD waits.)

DORA. You spoke to my father.

FREUD. What makes you think that?

DORA. He came home swearing at you one day.

FREUD. Did he? It appears I make you BOTH angry.

DORA. Didn't he convince you?

FREUD. Why are you so sure there's something improper in your father's relations with Frau Klippstein?

DORA. It's obvious.

FREUD. Make it obvious to ME.

DORA. It started with all that nursing.

FREUD. Why didn't your mother nurse him?

DORA. Mother hates any kind of disorder, dirt, messiness. Frau Klippstein is not so particular. Before she came along, he wouldn't let anybody nurse him but me.

FREUD. Then why did he switch to Frau Klippstein?

DORA. I suppose he wanted a more intimate kind of nursing.

FREUD. What evidence do you have they were intimate?

DORA. In the summer after my father's illness our two families took a suite of rooms at a resort hotel. One day Frau Klippstein, who was sharing a room with her little girl, announced at breakfast—

(DORA and FRAU K at the table, MARCY with the children up in the bedroom, WOLF has become the waiter.)

FRAU K. You know, Dora, I think perhaps we might do well to re-arrange our rooms. Little Grindl doesn't want her mommy sleeping with her any more. Isn't that sad?

DORA. I thought she loved sleeping with you.

FRAU K. Oh, she may say she does, but I think it would be very good for her to sleep without me. She's not a baby any more. We could put her in with Marcy.

MARCY. (*Holding Grindl up in the air, giggling.*) Wheeeeeee. Grindl can fly.

FRAU K. That would at least give them both something to do. God knows, for a governess, that girl doesn't do much governing. I'm not sure WHAT she does, except eat. She does that well. Such a fragile looking creature, and she eats like a soldier.

(MARCY is feeding Grindl, very tenderly.)

DORA. Will you sleep with your husband then?

FRAU K. What a silly girl. I wouldn't dream of that, he loves his privacy so. I'll just sleep in the vacant room at the end of the hall, that's the easiest thing, don't you think?

DORA. You could sleep in my room. It would save the extra money.

FRAU K. That's very sweet of you, dear, but I don't want to bother you.

DORA. It wouldn't bother me. It'd be fun, like when I was a little girl and stayed at your house.

FRAU K. You're still a little girl in many ways, Dora.

DORA. No I'm not.

FRAU K. Then as an adult, you must have your own room, and so must I. Look, here comes that wretched waiter, he always looks as if he'd just eaten the baby. What should we try for breakfast? Do you like squid?

DORA. *(To Freud.)* A day or two later my father began to plant not very subtle hints about the unsuitability of HIS room.

FATHER. It's got bats, for one thing, they fly around at night, and the draft is so bad, when my nose runs it freezes on my mustache, the chamber pot was frozen solid last night, and the man next door practices the tuba early in the morning, and he sneezes while he plays, it's not very nice at all. I've half a mind to move down to that other vacant room at the end of the hall.

DORA. This room and Frau Klippstein's new room were separated by a narrow passage only. It wasn't hard to see through this arrangement, of course, but they were so hot for each other, and they thought we were all so stupid—

(The first strains of the main waltz theme of The Blue Danube, *accompanied by dreadful tuba and punctuated at the end of each phrase by increasingly unfortunate sneezing. We hear the first 32 bars of this main waltz theme while watching people sneak in and out of rooms in some approximation of the following: measures 1-4: MOTHER hears a noise and goes into the hall and up the stairs; 5-8: WOLF, having snuck out for a rendezvous with Marcy, makes his way in the dark to the foot of the same stairs; 9-12: FRAU K makes her way up other stairs into the bedroom; 13-16: HERR K makes his way stealthily up the back steps of the bedroom; 17-20: MARCY getting out of bed and moving down another set of steps to look for Wolf; 21-*

24: FATHER moves up the central steps to the bedroom where, unbeknownst to him, HERR K has lain down to wait for somebody; 25-26: MOTHER backing down the steps and WOLF backing up the steps meet at the rumps and BOTH scream loudly; 27-28: FATHER encounters HERR K in bed, BOTH greatly startled, scream; 29-30: HERR K, having leaped out of bed, runs into MARCY on the steps, BOTH scream; 32: FATHER, running out of the bedroom, runs into the bewildered MARCY on the central steps, BOTH scream, and as the climactic notes of orchestra, tuba and ultimate sneeze resound, FATHER loses his balance on the steps, flails his arms and does a majestic belly flop onto the central stage, and EACH PERSON is back where they started.)

FREUD. Did no one else observe that these events were in any way peculiar?

DORA. When the same thing happened every summer, I finally brought it to Mother's attention myself.

(MOTHER is cleaning and humming The Blue Danube.*)*

DORA. Mother?

MOTHER. Hmm hmmmm hmmmmm Hmmmmm HMMMMMMMM—DOOT DOOT, DOOT DOOT.

DORA. MOTHER.

MOTHER. Don't bellow, dear, it makes your face purple.

DORA. Doesn't it bother you that Father spends so much time with Frau Klippstein?

MOTHER. Why should that bother me?

DORA. I asked him why, and he said I should be grateful for what she's done. What does that mean?

MOTHER. Dora, one day your father went into the woods, in great despair over his illness, determined to end his life, and Frau Klippstein, who happened to be passing by, stumbled upon him, and convinced him to reconsider for the sake of his children. You owe your father's life to her.

DORA. You believe that?

MOTHER. Yes, I believe it. I myself saw them walking from the woods that very day, and that's when your father explained it all to me. I embraced her like a sister.

DORA. Mother, you're pathetic.

MOTHER. I hope when you're older, Dora, you'll learn something about life and truth.

DORA. Why should I? You never did.

MOTHER. Yes, now you think you're smart and I'm stupid. When you're older perhaps you will be stupid like me and think the girl you are now even more stupid. Life is like this. Trust me, Dora. Truth is what you can deal with.

DORA. Life is not like this. I don't want life to be like this. Mother, don't the sleeping arrangements in this hotel disturb you just a little bit?

MOTHER. I sleep fine, dear. How do YOU sleep?

DORA. I'm so ashamed for you.

MOTHER. In this time and place, my love, we fight with those weapons we have. We learn this, or we die. Of course, we die anyway, but if we learn this, sometimes we die happier. So unless you want to go live with your Uncle Otto at the fruitcake farm, you'd better listen to your mother, all right? (*DORA won't look at her. MOTHER is sad for her.*) Ohhhhhhh. So stubborn. They don't like that. Poor baby. (*SHE gives Dora a kiss on the cheek and waltzes away sadly, humming, with her feather duster.*)

Scene 10

FREUD. I must admit this sounds a bit suspicious.

DORA. It was a disgrace. After we got home, every few weeks my father would cough—

(*FATHER coughs.*)

DORA. —and give us some story about how he must go back to the country for a while, for his health—

FATHER. (*Very plausibly.*) Blah blah blah blah, blah blah blah, blah blah.

DORA. Then he'd write back the most cheerful letters—

MOTHER. (*Reading the letter.*) Dear Munchkins, it says, how are you, I am fine, I hope you are all fine, I'm feeling much better now, I hope you are all feeling much better, I am feeling so VERY much better, oh, how much better I am feeling, yum yum, blah blah blah, blah blah, love and kisses to my sweetpie Dorry, your ever-loving Poppy. Isn't that sweet.

DORA. He was meeting Frau Klippstein, of course.

FREUD. You know this for certain?

DORA. She was always gone when he was gone. Frau Klippstein had been before this herself a rather sick woman—

(FRAU KLIPPSTEIN coughs.)

DORA. Bedridden.

FRAU K. Time for bed?

DORA. Whereas now she is merely ridden in bed.

FATHER. Dora, don't be vulgar.

DORA. Who taught me to be vulgar? You're the king of vulgarity.

FREUD. But now she's better?

DORA. She's incredibly robust and cheerful.

FRAU K. Push-ups? Tennis? Bull riding? Massage?

(WOLF, who is on the couch holding Mama's knitting, can't resist this offer, but MOTHER yanks him back firmly by the yarn.)

DORA. They were apparently a great tonic for each other. Herr Klippstein even complained to Mother about them spending so much time together.

MOTHER. Who, you and me?

HERR K. No, your wife and my husband. I mean, my husband and your wife.

DORA. Mother just hummed and dusted the credenza.

MOTHER. Shame on you for thinking such things.

HERR K. Maybe you and I should step out some time, what do you say?

MOTHER. Out? Step out? I don't step out. It's dirty out there. If one steps out, one may step into something. Stay home and cultivate your garden, you silly man.

DORA. One day my father came home with a big smile on his face and announced—

FATHER. Children, I have a big surprise for you—
we're moving to Vienna. You may kiss me now, Dora, on
the lips if you like, and jump up and down.

DORA. Isn't this rather sudden?

FATHER. Business, can't be helped.

DORA. Soon after this, the Klippsteins also moved to
Vienna, also business, no doubt the same business.

HERR K. Monkey business. Dog business.

DORA. And I began to see Father and Frau Klippstein
walking together with greater and greater regularity.
(*Coming upon them.*) Well, here we are again. I seem to
meet you two on the street every day since we all moved to
Vienna on business.

FATHER. My business takes me along a route which
Frau Klippstein frequents.

DORA. I'm sure it does.

FATHER. There's nothing mysterious about it.

DORA. Not to me.

FRAU K. It's a lovely day today, isn't it, Dora?

DORA. No it's not. For one thing, it smells.

FRAU K. It smells wonderful. It's spring, the colors
are coming out on bushes and vines, purple and yellow, red
and orange flowers, doesn't it excite you?

DORA. It stinks.

FRAU K. Why don't you let me introduce you to a nice
young man who—

DORA. Young men stink.

FRAU K. My, but you're a little ray of sunshine today.
If you'd just stop feeling sorry for yourself long enough
to—

FATHER. We've got to be getting along now, Dora. I've agreed to escort Frau Klippstein to the butcher on my way to Dr. Freud's. His office is just above there.

DORA. Oh, does Frau Klippstein nurse the butcher, too?

FATHER. Dora—

DORA. I'll tell Mother you'll be late for dinner.

FATHER. When am I ever late for dinner?

DORA. I thought you might want to be late for dinner.

FATHER. No, I like dinner.

DORA. Maybe Frau Klippstein would like to be late for HER dinner.

FRAU K. I'm never late. I come when it's time to come, and when I'm not wanted, I go. A lady must learn these things. And now I think it's time to go. I hope you have a pleasant day. Please smile for me, will you? No? Well, goodbye then.

(SHE kisses Dora on the cheek and THEY go. HERR K has been watching all this unobtrusively.)

HERR K. Charming couple, aren't they?

DORA. Are you following them, or me?

HERR K. I don't know what you mean.

DORA. It's a grotesque game of hide and seek we play. I run into them, and you're lurking under the lamp post. It's like a great, perverse dance.

(Softly, we hear Vienna Blood, *as if played by an organ grinder.)*

HERR K. You exaggerate.

DORA. Don't tell me I exaggerate. I have not yet begun to exaggerate. Fear me if I get to the point when I can no longer avoid exaggeration.

HERR K. Lower your voice, you're distracting people from the organ grinder, the monkey is jealous. Hello, monkey. Nice boy. I assure you I'm just out walking. Why are you so sensitive about this? Are you following them yourself? Or are you following me? Or are you perhaps meeting some young man on the sly, and just trying to draw our attention away from this?

DORA. You stupid man, do you think I'm as lecherous and pathetic as all of you are? I hate men, hate all of them, castrate them, CASTRATE THEM ALL.

(WOLF and MARCY are strolling by, shocked, and
MARCY puts Wolf's hat over his crotch as THEY back
away, just as a rich orchestra version of Vienna Blood
begins. FATHER and FRAU KLIPPSTEIN begin to
waltz. WOLF and MARCY waltz in great lovely
circles. MOTHER waltzes with the doll-child PETER.)

HERR K. Dora, may I have the pleasure of this dance?
DORA. No. I do NOT dance.
HERR K. Oh, come on, please, Dora, just one dance? Pretty please?
DORA. I DO NOT DANCE. I DO NOT DANCE. I DO NOT, DO NOT DANCE.

(DORA stands alone, fists clenched and furious, in the
midst of lovely swirling LIGHTS and DANCERS. The
WALTZ ends and the DANCERS drift away.)

Scene 11

FREUD. Why do you refuse to dance? Do you fear human contact?

DORA. I'm not afraid. I just don't like it.

FREUD. Doesn't Frau Klippstein dance?

DORA. Frau Klippstein is a wonderful dancer, and a very accomplished liar, always pretending she cares so much about me.

FATHER. She does care about you, and you care about her, you worship Frau Klippstein, you know you do.

DORA. I spit on Frau Klippstein, Frau Klippstein can kiss my foot, Frau Klippstein—

FRAU K. (*Appearing with flowers. DORA stops.*) I've just got some flowers, and I thought you might like some, I know how much you love them. (*SHE hands Dora the flowers.*)

DORA. (*Hesitates, then takes them.*) Thank you.

FRAU K. It seems a shame to pick them, but as my husband says, they were made for such things, if it isn't plucked it will just wither and die, so better it's at least enjoyed before it withers. I know he's right, but it makes me so sad, doesn't it make you sad, the way things are?

DORA. Yes.

FRAU K. Whatever you think of us, Dora, we love you very much, and we accept you as you are, and we hope you can love us and accept us as we are, too. Do you understand that? (*No response.*) Well, I should dress for dinner. Would you like to come help me?

DORA. Are you speaking to me or to Father?

FRAU K. To you, of course.

DORA. I've seen you dress. Of course, so has—

FATHER. She'll be along in just a moment.

FRAU K. All right. (*SHE smiles at Dora, looks away sadly and goes.*)

FATHER. You will not, I repeat, NOT speak disrespectfully of Frau Klippstein in or out of her presence ever again, or distress or hurt her in any way, is that clear?

DORA. Yes, general. May I polish your boots, general?

FATHER. Now go and help her dress.

DORA. She knows how to dress. She also knows how to undress, she's had so much practice. You won't break with them because you're in love with her.

FATHER. (*Glancing nervously towards MOTHER, who is playing with the Klippstein CHILDREN.*) Be quiet, your mother will hear.

DORA. Even when Mother hears, she doesn't hear. You and Frau Klippstein have made her this way.

FATHER. For the last time, Frau Klippstein is just my friend.

DORA. And I'm just your daughter, and therefore your property, to be used as you see fit.

FATHER. In fact I indulge you far too much. You're spoiled, you need discipline.

DORA. What I need is a decent and honest father who loves me.

(*Pause. FATHER is hurt, sits down.*)

DORA. I've hurt you. I'm sorry. I am. (*SHE comes over and sits in his lap, leans her head on his shoulder.*)

FATHER. Dora, I have something to explain to you Please listen and try to understand.

DORA. Are you going to tell me where babies come from?

FATHER. Dora.

DORA. All right, I'll be good. What is it?

FATHER. I think the cause of all your problems and mine too is your mother.

DORA. You ARE going to tell me where babies come from. Oh, goody.

FATHER. I have something important to tell you about your mother, so please listen to me.

DORA. Is she going to die? Or is it BAD news?

FATHER. Dora, your mother—(*Gravely.*)—is stupid.

MOTHER. (*Cuddling baby GRINDL and making noises.*) Lgl lgl lgl uggle.

DORA. (*Mock horror.*) Oh, my God, no.

FATHER. I'm afraid so.

DORA. Is there any cure?

FATHER. I don't think so.

DORA. Should we have her put to sleep?

FATHER. Why do I feel you're not taking this in the proper spirit?

DORA. Father, I've noticed that Mother is stupid. God, you don't think it's contagious, do you? What are the symptoms? (*Putting her hand on his forehead.*) Are you feverish? Do you have an uncontrollable urge to dust?

FATHER. Young ladies are not supposed to make jokes.

DORA. (*Getting up.*) Well, somebody's got to. You have no sense of humor any more. Mother's too stupid to know she's funny. Wolf's made himself into a fashionable doorstop, and I'm supposed to be Daddy's little pretzel, Mama's little wienerschnitzel, Papa's little lump of dung, mouth shut, legs together, sit up straight while Daddy sleeps with neighbor lady and her husband touches my body and says filthy things.

FATHER. Dora, this behavior is unnatural.

DORA. It certainly is.

FATHER. I need someone to talk to, I get so lonely I think I'd go out of my mind if I lost her friendship.

DORA. So you'd rather have ME go out of MY mind instead? If you want somebody to talk to, talk to ME.

FATHER. It's not the same thing.

DORA. I know. For one thing, she's got much larger breasts.

FATHER. Dora, go to your room.

DORA. This is my room.

FATHER. Then go to MY room.

DORA. Frau Klippstein is in your room. Let me alone, I can't breathe, I feel faint—

FREUD. No you don't.

DORA. I know when I feel faint.

FREUD. All right, go on then, faint.

DORA. I can't faint on cue.

FREUD. I'll bet you can if you try.

DORA. That's absurd.

FREUD. I thought you felt faint.

DORA. I did feel faint.

FREUD. But you don't now. You see? I was right.

DORA. What an impossible man you are.

FREUD. Why do you make it so difficult for your father? He was at least trying to explain things to you, to treat you as an adult, and you rejected him.

DORA. He rejected me. He lied to me.

FREUD. You won't let him tell the truth. You don't want to understand.

DORA. Do you deny that he tries to mold my view of what's real to suit his own ends? Or that he's got an understanding with Herr Klippstein to overlook assaults on me as long as his relations with Frau Klippstein are also overlooked?

FREUD. You think there's some formal agreement to this effect?

DORA. Oh, no, they'd never be so open as that, that's the scary part, they're just careful to avoid drawing any inconvenient conclusions. Herr Klippstein sent me flowers every day for months and nobody said anything.

MOTHER. (*Coming in with flowers.*) More snapdragons, pussy willows, pansies, passion flowers, all from Herr Klippstein, what a sweet man. How lucky we are to have him for a friend. Smell. (*SHE sticks the flowers in Dora's face.*)

DORA. (*Sneezing loudly.*) AAAAAACHHOOOOO.

MOTHER. Gesundheit. Catching a chill. It's all those walks you take, and also sleeping in the nude, shame on you, go right to bed.

DORA. And my father gives valuable presents to Frau Klippstein and my parents profess to see nothing unusual in this.

MOTHER. (*Arranging flowers and humming "The Blue Danube."*) Hmm hmmm hmmm hmmmm HMMMMM— DOOT DOOT, DOOT DOOT.

DORA. Mother, he's given her a diamond brooch, a rhododendron, a small dog, a complete encyclopedia, four rings, three necklaces and a parrot. Don't you find that the least bit odd?

MOTHER. Yes, I'll tell you, Dora, it does seem odd, I can't imagine what she'd want with a parrot, they talk like sailors, they peck at your titties, and they poop all over the sofa, just like your uncle Otto.

FREUD. A string of reproaches towards others, especially those we love, whether true or false, leads one to suspect a similar string of self-reproaches in the speaker, with the same content.

DORA. What on earth are you talking about? What language is that? Nobody talks like that.

FREUD. You reproach others to divert suspicion from yourself.

DORA. Suspicion of what?

FREUD. Did you always resent your father's friendship with Frau Klippstein?

DORA. Not at first. But when I realized what was going on—

FREUD. Before or after Herr Klippstein's behavior at the lake?

DORA. I was much angrier at them after that, but—

FREUD. Before the lake, did you sometimes avoid going to see Frau Klippstein when you thought your father was there?

DORA. Should I have gone to watch?

FREUD. Did you want to watch?

DORA. So what if I wasn't so angry with them until after Herr Klippstein attacked me at the lake, what does that prove?

FREUD. That your feelings about these two things are connected in some very important way. Perhaps you accuse your father and Frau Klippstein of just what you wanted to happen between you and her husband.

DORA. That is absolute garbage.

FREUD. The violence of your reaction proves we've touched a nerve.

DORA. WE HAVE NOT TOUCHED A NERVE. *(SHE stands there, trembling and upset, looking at him.)* All right. We've touched a nerve. But I'm not sure what nerve we've touched. Are you?

FREUD. What did you dream last night?

DORA. I didn't dream last night. Well, maybe I did. Why?

FREUD. If you want to know what nerve we've touched, tell me your dream.

Scene 12

(Eerie version of "Vienna Blood" and a THUNDERSTORM approaching as the stage begins DARKENING to what will become a hellish RED LIGHT, and DORA moves uncertainly up towards the bed as SHE begins to remember.)

DORA. I dreamed there was a thunderstorm, and I was in bed, and it was very warm, and my father came into my room and was shaking me.

(SHE's in bed in the eerie RED LIGHT. FATHER has rushed up in his nightcap to shake her.)

FATHER. Dora? Wake up.
DORA. What is it? What's the matter?

FATHER. The house is on fire. It's burning. Everything is burning. Get up and get dressed, quickly.

DORA. But I want to stay in bed.

FATHER. Get up. Come quickly. It's burning.

DORA. (*Trying to cover herself.*) All right. I'm hurrying. Don't look. Don't look.

MOTHER. (*In nightcap, running madly around in circles with her duster and a great stack of doilies.*) Wait. Stop. We can't go yet.

FATHER. But the house is burning.

MOTHER. SAVE MY JEWEL CASE. I MUST SAVE MY JEWEL CASE.

FATHER. FOR CHRIST SAKE, WOMAN, THE HOUSE IS ON FIRE.

MOTHER. THAT'S WHY I MUST SAVE MY JEWEL CASE.

FATHER. I WILL NOT LET MY CHILDREN BURN UP LIKE TOAST FOR THE SAKE OF YOUR STUPID JEWEL CASE. WHO NEEDS YOUR JEWEL CASE? WHAT GOOD IS IT?

DORA. I'm coming as fast as I can.

FATHER. Down the stairs and out the door, down the stairs and out the door, it's burning, burning.

DORA. (*As the RED LIGHT and THUNDERSTORM begin to fade.*) We rushed downstairs, and as soon as I was outside, I woke up. I don't see what help a dream can be.

FREUD. It's a kind of detour by which certain dangerous knowledge can be passed through but evaded at the same time. The mind uses symbols like a poet. If we can read the symbols, we can see deep into your soul. Had you had this dream before?

DORA. At the lake, just after the incident with Herr Klippstein. Then every night for a while. Then again last night.

FREUD. That means we're doing good work. Now think back through the dream and tell me when it puts you in mind of anything, no matter how trivial it may seem.

DORA. Father's been arguing with Mother because she insists on locking the dining room door when she goes to bed.

MOTHER. We've always locked it. My mother locked it. My grandmother locked it.

FATHER. But Wolf's room has no separate entrance. What if something should happen in the night, and he needs to leave?

MOTHER. What could happen? The boy has a chamber pot.

DORA. I thought, if there's a fire, my brother will die because the door is locked.

FREUD. Good. What else?

DORA. (*Making her way back to the bed.*) When we got to the lake there was a thunderstorm, and when Father saw the wooden house with no lightning rod he said he was afraid of fire. I went to lie down in Frau Klippstein's bedroom, and woke up suddenly, and Herr Klippstein was standing over me like my father in the dream.

(During what follows, MARCY takes the CHILDREN to the dock and dangles her bare legs in the water.)

HERR K. You look very nice when you're asleep.
DORA. What are you doing here?

HERR K. This is my wife's bedroom. Certainly I'm allowed in my wife's bedroom, at least when my wife's not here.

DORA. What do you want?

HERR K. That's a rather broad question.

DORA. Why are you here?

HERR K. There's something I need.

DORA. What is it?

HERR K. What do you think it is?

DORA. Excuse me. (*SHE tries to get past him.*)

HERR K. Wait. What's the matter? I've lost something, is all.

DORA. What have you lost?

HERR K. I can't remember. I didn't mean to frighten you. I just—

(HE notices for the first time that FRAU KLIPPSTEIN is watching them from the doorway.)

HERR K. Oh, hello. I was just—looking for something.

FRAU K. I know you were.

HERR K. Perhaps I should look elsewhere. I frightened Dora. Sometimes when you wake up suddenly you get disoriented. At least I do. I'm going out to feed the ducks. Or the children. Maybe I'll take the children to feed the ducks. Maybe I'll feed the children to the ducks. I don't know. Who cares? (*HE goes away.*)

DORA. Is there a key to the bedroom?

FRAU K. I suppose there is. Why do you ask?

DORA. I don't like to be disturbed.

FRAU K. He won't disturb you. He's harmless.

DORA. I don't think he's harmless.

FRAU K. Suppose you lock it and I want to come in and lie down?

DORA. You can knock and I'll let you in.

FRAU K. That will spoil your nap.

DORA. I don't care. Please give me the key.

FRAU K. (*Giving Dora a large key.*) All right, but be careful with it, it's the only one.

DORA. (*To Freud.*) The next morning I locked myself in while I was dressing, but in the afternoon when I went to lie down, the key was gone. I know Herr Klippstein took it. After that I was terrified he'd surprise me, so I dressed very quickly. I felt especially uneasy because Frau Klippstein often took long walks with my father, and I'd be left alone in the house with Herr Klippstein.

(Ticking CLOCK. DORA sits reading. HERR K watches.)

HERR K. Would you like a cookie?

DORA. No thank you. Haven't they come back yet?

HERR K. Why should they? There's nothing for them here. They've abandoned us. Don't you feel abandoned?

DORA. Where is Marcy?

HERR K. Out with the children. They seem to be having a good time. I'm glad somebody is. Your father and my wife are also having a good time. And you and I sit home lonely and miserable.

DORA. I'm very happy.

HERR K. Do you know what I'm going to do?

DORA. No. What?

HERR K. I'm going to have a cookie.

(DORA pretends to concentrate on her book, trembling. HE is very close, hands on the back of her chair, and has just begun to bend down towards her when MARCY runs in from the dock, excited and happy.)

MARCY. DUCKS.

(HERR K and DORA both jump.)

DORA. *(Getting up abruptly.)* Pardon me?

MARCY. There's ducks by the dock. The children are in heaven. Come and see.

DORA. I'd love to.

HERR K. You leave the children alone by the water?

MARCY. I can see them from here. They're perfectly—

HERR K. Don't ever leave my children alone by the water, do you understand?

MARCY. But it's all right, they're just—

HERR K. DO YOU UNDERSTAND?

MARCY. Yes sir.

(HE storms out. MARCY starts to cry.)

DORA. Don't cry, it's all right, I'm sure he didn't mean to—

MARCY. Of course he did. Excuse me. *(SHE runs back to the children.)*

FREUD. *(Looking at Marcy, thoughtful.)* This governess, Marcy, did she perhaps—

DORA. *(Getting quickly between Freud and Marcy.)* Herr Klippstein gave me a jewel case like the one in the dream.

FREUD. Did he? Do you know that jewel case is a crude name for the female genitals?

DORA. That's quaint. And just before the dream, my parents had an argument about jewelry.

MOTHER. I want pearl drops for my ears, what's wrong with that?

FATHER. I don't like women with things hanging out their ears. Why can't you just take the bracelet and be satisfied?

MOTHER. I don't like bracelets, they jingle when I dust and scratch the furniture.

FATHER. Then don't wear it when you dust.

MOTHER. If you insist on spending good money on something I don't want, you'd better find somebody else to give it to.

(DORA's eyes light up and SHE holds out her hand.)

FATHER. All right. I will. I'll give it to Frau Klippstein.

(DORA pulls her hand back.)

FREUD. So you thought, Herr Klippstein is persecuting me—

DORA. Like Dr. Freud does.

FREUD. He wants to force his way into my—room, so to speak.

DORA. Like you force your way into my mind.

FREUD. You thought, my jewel case is in danger, and it's my father's fault for walking with Frau Klippstein when he should be here protecting me, which is just what he was doing in your dream. And you wanted to take the gift your mother rejected. He got nothing from her. You were willing to give him something.

DORA. I wanted to give my father my jewel case?

FREUD. You wanted to give Herr Klippstein your jewel case.

DORA. I'm awfully free with my jewel case, aren't I?

FREUD. You summoned up your childish love for your father to protect yourself from your attraction to Herr Klippstein. The dream says you're ready to give him what he wants. You're not so much afraid of Herr Klippstein as of yourself. You're afraid you'll give in to him.

DORA. Oh, that's just stupid. I'm going home.

FREUD. Yes, you run away because we're getting close to the truth, and because the return of your dream last night means you're now developing a similar conflict with me.

DORA. With you?

FREUD. I'm afraid so.

DORA. In short, I'm quite a slut.

FREUD. Nonsense. It's called transference. Your father makes you come here. I'm in part replacing both him and Herr Klippstein in your mind. The analyst comes to embody everything the patient wants and is afraid of. If you leave now, you prove I'm right.

DORA. WHAT AN ARROGANT, INFURIATING MAN YOU ARE.

FREUD. Yes, I know, I know.

(THEY look at each other. FREUD smiles very engagingly at her and shrugs.)

DORA. I don't believe any of that.

FREUD. Yes you do. We simply trace the effect back to the cause, and where there is smoke, there must always be fire.

DORA. Smoke. I smelled smoke, each time I woke up, at the lake. What does that mean? That I wanted a cigar?

FREUD. Your father smokes heavily. So does Herr Klippstein.

DORA. And so do you.

FREUD. And so do I. Herr Klippstein offered you a cigarette before his unfortunate proposal. A kiss from a smoker would smell of smoke.

DORA. You smell like smoke right now. Do I want you to kiss me?

FREUD. I don't know. Do you?

(THEY look at each other.)

DORA. This transference, does it work both ways?

FREUD. How do you mean?

DORA. As I become emotionally involved with my analyst, does he become emotionally involved with me?

FREUD. Not if he's good, no.

DORA. Why not? He's a person, too, isn't he? He was a child once, too, wasn't he? He needs things just like his patients, doesn't he?

FREUD. The analyst is not neurotic.

DORA. *(Furious.)* Oh, I see. How silly of me. *(SHE takes a cigar out of his cigar box and begins shredding it and throwing pieces at him as SHE speaks, her anger building considerably as she goes on.)* Well, I've had enough for today, thank you. I don't want to hang around you too long at one time, or I might not be able to control myself, my neurotic passions might just overwhelm me, and I might just jump on you like a sex-crazed baboon. We've got your professional virtue to think of, don't we, sweetie? You've got to watch us neurotic women, you never know what we'll do next, do you? (*SHE throws one last wad of cigar in his face and storms away, stopping with her back to him upstage.*)

FREUD. No, I don't. (*HE wipes cigar shreds off his suit.*) But I have hopes.

(*A rich, luxuriant version of the main waltz theme of "Vienna Blood" is heard. HERR KLIPPSTEIN asks Dora to dance. SHE refuses. FATHER and FRAU KLIPPSTEIN dance. WOLF and MARCY dance. MOTHER dances with her duster. Swirling LIGHTS fading as FREUD lights his cigar, the PEOPLE dance off, and FREUD and DORA look at each other from across the stage as the LIGHTS go out and the MUSIC ends. End of Act I.*)

ACT II

Scene 13

We hear "Tales from the Vienna Woods," the first 109 measures, through to the end of the first zither section, as the people enter as follows: measures 1-15, LIGHTS up slowly; 16-56, FREUD enters, inspects this world, thinking, culminating in the long final note of this section, on which FRAU K steps into view and HER eyes meet Freud's; 57-65, SHE crosses up to the bedroom, FREUD watching her; 66-72, HERR K enters from the same spot, tracing her path up to the bedroom steps, where SHE turns away from him; the long, trilling bird-like measure 73 and its conclusion in 74 are MARCY's entrance, in her robe and barefoot, sad; on the three measures that introduce the zither section (75-77) HERR K and MARCY share a look across the stage which is chilling, ambiguous and unpleasant, and then as the soft zither section begins (78) MARCY makes a long, sad cross to the window (78-85), and looks out, lost. On measure 86, when the phrase repeats, WOLF appears, moves to Marcy as if to comfort her, but at the little climax of measure 89 sees FATHER approaching, stops, turns reluctantly away from her and goes to the sofa, sitting down at the end of Father's entrance (90-93). The moderato section (94-101) is MOTHER's happy dusting entrance—SHE stops at Marcy, moves to comfort her, thinks better of it, and sits on the windowseat as DORA appears on the steps (102-109)

*and looks at Freud from across the stage. The MUSIC
ends and the PEOPLE freeze briefly for the second
photograph, the essence of which is private suffering,
and then the scene begins, WOLF reading the paper on
the sofa. As the scene progresses, the PEOPLE all go
about their business as in the first act.*

WOLF. (*Turning away from MARCY, whose eyes
meet his as SHE goes off past him to dress. To Dora:*) So,
how's it going with Dr. Freud? You spend an awful lot of
time there. Is he any good?

DORA. He's unexpectedly engaging, in an infuriating
kind of way. Have you heard from Marcy lately?

WOLF. What do you and Freud do, anyway?

DORA. We talk. Mostly about Father and Frau
Klippstein.

WOLF. God, what for?

DORA. I don't know. I can't seem to help it. Have you
and Marcy—

WOLF. If you want my opinion, we're not Father's
keeper. Be glad he's got somebody to talk to. Mother
doesn't seem to care, and they're too old to do anything.
Have some pity on the old boy.

DORA. They're not old at all, and I'd like to agree with
you about it, but I can't, I can't forgive them.

WOLF. For what?

DORA. Wolf, I know they didn't want you seeing her,
but if you really care about her—

WOLF. I don't want to talk about it, and I think you
should stay away from that Freud person, it's costing Dad a
fortune and it's making you weird.

DORA. I wasn't weird before?

WOLF. Yes, but this is worse.

DORA. Do you think I'm crazy?

WOLF. No, I think Freud's crazy. He hangs around with people like Uncle Otto all the time, what do you expect?

DORA. I don't know if he's crazy, but he says the most outrageous things, and he's so frustrating, he's always contradicting me—

FREUD. I never contradict you.

DORA. You're doing it now.

FREUD. No I'm not. You accuse me of your own symptom. The contrary is always asserted.

DORA. No it isn't. What?

FREUD. You want to hide something so you shout loudly its opposite.

DORA. NO I DON'T.

(FREUD grins. DORA gives up in frustration.)

DORA. So how do we rid me of this curse?

FREUD. We bring what's hidden to the surface. The roots of your obsession lie deep in your unconscious. Your behavior goes far beyond normal daughterly concern. You feel and act like a jealous wife, you put yourself in your mother's place—

(MOTHER tries to give Dora her duster.)

FREUD. And when you faint in your father's arms and sit on his lap, you put yourself in Frau Klippstein's place—

(FRAU KLIPPSTEIN gives Dora a rose.)

FREUD. You identify with the woman your father once loved and the woman he now loves. In fact, you're in love with him.

DORA. That's horrible.

FREUD. No it's not, it's a kind of ghost from everybody's infancy, but it's much more intense in those marked for neurosis, who develop prematurely and have an abnormal craving for love, like you. Your father was proud of your intelligence and beauty, and made you his confidante, even as a child, and his illness drew you even closer. It was you and not your mother that Frau Klippstein replaced.

DORA. Is that why Mother hates me? For the same reason I hate Frau Klippstein? Because I took Father away from her?

FREUD. You're getting very good at this, you know.

DORA. Poor Mother. My cousin told me once she hoped to marry her father when her mother was dead.

FREUD. Your unconscious has just answered yes to our question by bringing that into your mind.

DORA. Maybe my unconscious is saying, no, my cousin was like that, but I'm not.

FREUD. The unconscious does not say no.

DORA. Maybe it should.

FREUD. You don't accept my explanation?

DORA. No.

FREUD. But you see, in this case, no means yes.

DORA. No means yes?

FREUD. Yes.

DORA. By that you mean no?

FREUD. No, I mean yes.

DORA. When I say no it means yes, but when you say no it means no?

FREUD. Well, yes and no.

DORA. Because I'm a woman?

FREUD. Because you're neurotic. You're incapable of seeing the situation objectively.

DORA. And you are?

FREUD. I'm not emotionally involved. You were close to Frau Klippstein, helped the growing intimacy between her and your father, and you clearly found Herr Klippstein attractive—

DORA. No I didn't.

FREUD. Yet when he made advances, you reacted violently, began to hate Frau Klippstein and became unreasonable about your father's friendship with her.

DORA. You find their friendship reasonable?

FREUD. I find it understandable. Beyond that it's not for me to judge.

DORA. But you judge ME, you do it all the time, you think you understand when you don't, and then you pass judgements.

FREUD. I try out answers. For example, suppose this: disturbed by your sexual feelings for Herr Klippstein, you reject him by reawakening feelings for your father which have slumbered since childhood, and thus you resent Frau Klippstein doubly—because she enjoys the favors of both men. How's that?

DORA. Prove it.

FREUD. I can prove it, but you've got to tell me the truth.

DORA. I'll tell you the truth.

FREUD. No matter what I ask. It may get very rough.

DORA. I can take it if you can.

FREUD. All right.

DORA. All right. Fire away.

FREUD. Did Herr Klippstein ever make any sexual advances towards you before the incident at the lake?

DORA. No.

FREUD. Truth.

DORA. No. Well, actually, yes. A long time ago. When I was fourteen.

FREUD. What happened when you were fourteen?

Scene 14

Calliope "Vienna Blood," softly. EERIE, DARK CARNIVAL atmosphere. WOLF takes MARCY to the carnival as the scene progresses.

DORA. We were going to the carnival. I was to meet the Klippsteins at his office, but when I got there, it seemed deserted. The door was unlocked, so I went up the stairs. I was frightened, it was getting dark, and I could hear the carnival music from down the street.

HERR K. (*Appearing on the steps above her.*) Dora?

DORA. Oh, you scared me. Where is everybody?

HERR K. I gave them the rest of the day off to go to the carnival. Wasn't that nice of me?

DORA. Where is your wife?

HERR K. She wasn't feeling well, so she stayed home in bed. It's just you and me. I didn't mean to startle you.

DORA. I don't like empty rooms. I dream about old houses.

HERR K. Poor Dora, so pretty, and so frail and timid. I'll protect you. (*HE is moving closer.*)

DORA. I'm not frail, and I'm not timid, and I don't need protection, I just have bad dreams.

HERR K. There's nothing for us to fear in this life, we must simply get through it as best we can, taking whatever simple pleasures turn up, don't you think?

DORA. I don't know. Yes, I think that's true.

HERR K. I'm glad you agree. (*HE puts his hands around her waist and pulls her gently but firmly towards him.*)

DORA. What are you doing?

HERR K. You know what this is. This is called a kiss. (*HE kisses her on the lips, passionately but not roughly, holding her tight against him.*)

DORA. (*Trying to pull away.*) Please—

HERR K. It's all right. This is something adults do to amuse themselves on rainy days. It's harmless, believe me.

DORA. I don't find it amusing.

HERR K. You will, eventually.

(*HE looks at her a moment, then smiles and allows HER to pull away a step or two.*)

HERR K. What's the matter? Don't you want to grow up?

(*WOLF and MARCY have returned from the carnival and SHE has a kewpie doll he's won for her. During the following HE kisses her goodnight, very innocently, and SHE runs in and sits on the sofa, happy, with kewpie doll.)*

DORA. Yes, but not so fast, I think.
HERR K. I've kissed you before.
DORA. Not like that.
HERR K. I didn't hurt you, did I?
DORA. No.
HERR K. Then what was so bad about it? Could it be that what you feel when I kiss you now is what's different?
DORA. Maybe.
HERR K. Then if the change is inside YOU, I'm not to blame, am I?
DORA. Am I to blame?
HERR K. No one's to blame. This is just life.
DORA. I think life is disgusting then.
HERR K. No you don't.

(HE touches her arm and SHE runs down the steps to Freud's office. When SHE touches the desk, the calliope MUSIC stops and the LIGHTS return to normal, but Freud isn't there, HE's behind her, and he startles her when he speaks.)

FREUD. You felt no sexual excitement at this moment?
DORA. Of course not.
FREUD. It's nothing to be ashamed of. We all have these feelings.
DORA. No, I did not feel sexual excitement when as a fourteen year old girl I was assaulted by the middle-aged husband of my father's mistress. What I felt was disgust.

FREUD. Why disgust? At that age girls are very much aware of sexual feelings. He's an attractive man—he must have been more so four years ago.

DORA. How do you know he's attractive?

FREUD. I met him once.

DORA. And have you spoken with him?

FREUD. Briefly.

DORA. About me?

FREUD. Of course not.

DORA. And you found him attractive?

FREUD. Well, he seems to me to—

DORA. If you find him so attractive why don't YOU go kiss him and tell me if YOU feel sexually excited.

FREUD. Disgust is a very strong word, one doesn't use it every day, especially in affairs of the heart. Disgust is more likely to be associated with functions of the anus. Might you have felt that his kiss was not so much a stimulation of your sex organs as an arousal of your anus?

DORA. Dr. Freud, do you take drugs?

FREUD. Not any more, why?

DORA. You seem to be suffering from the most bizarre delusions about human motivation. Just what world are you living in?

FREUD. I hope the same one as you, but a different state of mind is sometimes like a different universe, and in some ways a healthy man can't hope to understand a sick one.

DORA. Then how can you pretend to understand me? I'm a woman, for God's sake. Are we even of the same species?

FREUD. When he kissed you, did he press his body against you?

DORA. He held me so tight, sometimes I can still feel him.

FREUD. Now? At this moment?

DORA. When I was telling you about it.

FREUD. What part of your body?

DORA. The upper part.

FREUD. Your breasts?

DORA. The upper part of my body.

FREUD. Not the lower part?

DORA. I don't remember the lower part.

FREUD. Do you know what a penis is?

DORA. Are you going to show me one?

FREUD. Many girls pretend ignorance on this subject.

DORA. Do you ask many girls this question? I hope you don't do this on the street.

FREUD. I presume the answer is yes. And from your earlier remarks about castration—

DORA. No, I don't know what a penis is, nor do I know what testicles are, so there's no use asking. I'm just an innocent young thing. Can we open a window? I'm suffocating.

FREUD. Do you often feel this way when alone in a room with a man?

DORA. I feel this way when I can't breathe.

FREUD. Do you fear, when alone with a man, that he may be sexually excited by you?

DORA. Are you sexually excited by me?

FREUD. When Herr Klippstein kissed you, did you feel your breath being taken away?

DORA. It WAS taken away. The man has a mouth like a suction cup.

FREUD. Do you know what happens to a man's body when he becomes stimulated sexually?

DORA. Has no one ever explained this to you?

FREUD. No, you explain it to me.

DORA. I believe his prick becomes stiff as a poker.

(Freud's CIGAR sags momentarily, but HE rallies and tries to cover by writing something.)

FREUD. *(Writing.)* I see.

DORA. *(Spelling it helpfully.)* P-r-i-

FREUD. Yes, I know, thank you. Have you seen men's sexual equipment?

DORA. I beg your pardon?

FREUD. On social occasions, when men sit on sofas, have you observed the outline of their sex organs through their trousers?

DORA. All the time.

(SHE looks pointedly at Freud's midsection. HE crosses his legs.)

FREUD. Do you have fantasies about the lower parts of men's bodies?

DORA. I don't know what you mean.

FREUD. Fantasies.

HERR K. *(Brandishing a long, floppy sausage.)* Would you like, before we go to the carnival, to enjoy a long, floppy sausage?

DORA. No thank you.

HERR K. I raised it myself. Would you like to touch it?

DORA. Disgusting.

HERR K. Go on, it won't bite you, if you don't bite it.

DORA. (*Hesitates, then touches the sausage.*) Well ... oooooooh.

HERR K. Oooooh. Would you like a bite?

DORA. Normal girls don't bite on men's sausages.

HERR K. Some do. It's a perfectly nice sausage, a very attractive sausage, I take good care of it, I only take it out on Sundays and special occasions—not like your father, who's got bumps all over HIS sausage. Any normal girl would die to place her moist lips for a moment to the tip of my sausage.

DORA. But it's meat, it's made of meat. Meat is disgusting.

HERR K. This is life, Dora. People are meat.

DORA. People are disgusting. Everything they do is disgusting.

HERR K. But Dora, my sausage is not like that, my sausage is spiritual, divine, transcendental, my sausage can SING.

WOLF. (*Entering in old-fashioned bathing costume, with beach umbrella, another floppy sausage stuffed in his suit to suggest exaggerated privates in surreal relief, sings:*)

Oh, sweet is the maiden and sweet is the hill
upon which I lay down and love did fulfill—

WOMEN. (*EXCEPT DORA, chorus.*) And love did fulfill.

FATHER and WOLF. (*As FATHER turns his back and urinates loudly into a bucket—use seltzer bottle:*)

Oh, sweet is the river that flows in its bed,
the river where my love's sweet soul swiftly sped—

WOMEN. Sweet soul swiftly sped.

HERR K, FATHER and WOLF. (*As HERR K conducts with his sausage.*)

And sweet is the wild wood, home of the tall tree,
the wild wood will stand strong, and bring my love to me.

WOMEN. And bring my love to me.

ALL. (*But DORA and FREUD.*)
THE WILD WOOD WILL STAND STRONG, HOME OF THE TALL TREE,
AND THE RIVER WILL CARRRYYYYYY MY TRUE LOVE HOME TO MEEE,

(*Big finish, very stirring:*)
MY TRUE LOVE HOME TOOOO ME
MY TRUE LOVE HOME
TOOOOOOOOO
MEEEEEEEEEE.

DORA. (*To Freud, as the SINGERS hold their final pose.*) No, I do NOT have sexual fantasies.

(*Hearing this, the assembled SINGERS sadly disband with sighs of disappointment, and HERR K goes forlornly away, his sausage now drooping.*)

Scene 15

FREUD. But you seem very well informed about sexual functions. Where did you learn about them?

DORA. Do we have to talk dirty all the time?

FREUD. We're translating from the unconscious to the conscious.

DORA. Isn't that dangerous?

FREUD. It's more dangerous when it stays unconscious. When we act from unconscious motives we're often irrational or even violent. If we make the motive conscious we have a chance to deal with it.

DORA. Aren't you afraid you're corrupting an innocent young girl?

FREUD. If she's really innocent, I can't corrupt her, and if she's not innocent, she's already corrupted. Did your mother tell you about the sexual act?

DORA. Mother was too busy sterilizing the piano.

FREUD. Did you have a governess who explained such things to you?

DORA. We had one, but I had her fired.

FREUD. For teaching you about sex?

DORA. For having impure thoughts about Father.

FREUD. How did you know what she was thinking?

DORA. She talked about him constantly. She looked at him like a wild goat. She was always dropping things and bending over in his presence. She was nice to me when he was around, but when he was gone she ignored me completely.

FREUD. And you resented this indifference.

DORA. I resented the duplicity.

FREUD. Didn't you have the same relationship to the Klippstein children as your governess had to you?

DORA. They had their own governess, Marcy.

(MARCY is in the bedroom playing with the children.)

FREUD. But you helped take care of them.

DORA. I'm very fond of them.

FREUD. The way your governess was fond of you?

DORA. What does that mean?

FREUD. I gather Herr Klippstein stayed with his wife for the sake of his children, perhaps the same reason your father stayed with your mother. This love for his children was something you and Herr Klippstein had in common, wasn't it?

DORA. So?

FREUD. Did you pretend to love the Klippstein children for the same reason your governess pretended to love you?

DORA. I wasn't pretending.

FREUD. What did Marcy think about you and Herr Klippstein? She was in an excellent position to observe you.

MARCY. Why do you look at him that way?

DORA. Look at who?

MARCY Herr Klippstein. Even when you don't look at him, you do it on purpose. You're wild about him, aren't you?

DORA. I certainly am not. What a ridiculous girl you are.

MARCY I can tell, Dora. You'd better be careful. In some ways, you know, he isn't really a very nice person.

DORA. In what ways? How do you know?

MARCY. (*Starts to say something, then thinks better of it.*) I've got to go wash the baby.

(SHE *turns to go,* FREUD *watching her, about to ask another question about her, when once again* DORA *gets between them.*)

DORA. All right, between the incident in the office and the one at the lake I might have had one or two girlish thoughts about Herr Klippstein, but never after the lake.

FREUD. He said his wife told him you were reading books about sex at the lake.

DORA. She would know. She was the one who read them to me.

FRAU K. (*Reading:*) "She sank down into the warm bath and felt his strong arms press her bare flesh to his, and a great shudder began to sweep through her adorable white body and deep into her soul. He kissed her breasts passionately—"

DORA. I won't listen to this filth, not a moment longer, not for five minutes longer. Perhaps for one minute. If you insist. But I'll listen with one ear covered.

FRAU K. "She felt him lift her up, and with one swift, shocking lunge he had penetrated between—" (*SHE continues to read silently, moving her finger rapidly across the page and mumbling.*)

DORA. Well, if you MUST read this trash, at least have the common decency to read it out loud.

FREUD. So it was Frau Klippstein who introduced you to sex.

DORA. I have to go now, I've got a stomach ache.

FREUD. Do you?

DORA. I have a stomach ache. People get stomach aches.

FREUD. Name one person you know who's recently had a stomach ache.

DORA. My cousin Gretchen. But she was faking. Her sister got engaged and Gretchen, who is a great, stupid baby and a jealous and selfish person, suddenly developed stomach pains just—(*SHE looks at Freud and realizes what she's saying.*)—to get attention. Coincidence.

FREUD. There's no such animal. So what happened to Gretchen?

DORA. Her parents fussed over her and sent her to a health resort. Her lover had deserted her just before her sister got engaged.

FREUD. And now you develop your own stomach pains. You identify with the rejected girl, who suffers pains like childbirth in jealousy over somebody else's good fortune. Do you see?

DORA. Well, Frau Klippstein pretends she's sick to keep from sleeping with her husband. It was a joke between us that when he'd come back from one of his business trips she'd get sick, and when he left again, she'd feel better and I'd get sick.

FREUD. And you were often sick when your father was off with Frau Klippstein. You threatened to die, in effect, if he didn't stop seeing her and spend time with you instead.

DORA. But I was really sick. I threw up.

FREUD. I'm sure you did. Sometimes we get so used to being sick it becomes a comfort to us, we cling to it, are frightened without it, resent all attempts to help. The disease becomes our only defense and finally our one reason for living. You don't want to be like that.

DORA. Doesn't it cheapen reality a bit when you're clever enough to prove anything you want? It makes truth a kind of parlor game.

FREUD. If I'm wrong then why do I make you so angry? A reproach that misses the mark can give no lasting offense, because it doesn't really threaten us.

DORA. A reproach that misses the mark may hit ANOTHER mark and give enormous offense by the very smugness and patronization with which it's spoken. This has nothing to do with sickness, it has to do with self-respect. I get angry because I'm not taken seriously as a person. What if I tell you that all your theories are absolute rot, that you've made them up so you can defend yourself from people like me?

FREUD. It doesn't bother me because I know it's not true.

DORA. But why does everything have to mean what you want it to mean? Can't it also mean something else?

FREUD. Truth is complex, but so are lies, especially the lies of an extraordinarily intelligent and gifted person like you. I must be careful, too, Dora, careful not to let you charm me away from the truth.

DORA. Do I charm you?

FREUD. What did you dream last night?

DORA. What did YOU dream? Did you dream about me?

FREUD. Tell me your dream. You're not afraid to tell me, are you?

(DORA looks at him, hesitates, remembering. MUSIC, faintly, eerie, "Vienna Blood.")

Scene 16

(STROBE effect and distorted CALLIOPE waltz.)

DORA. *(Walking among the others.)* I'm walking in a strange town, the streets are unfamiliar. On one square

there's a monument. (*FATHER is the monument.*) I come
to the house where I live, go to my room, and find a letter
from my mother.

MOTHER. Dear Dora, As you have left home without
your parents' knowledge, I have not written to tell you
your father is sick. Now, however, you may come if you
like, question mark, as your father is dead. Yours truly,
Mummy.

DORA. I go outside and try to find my way to the
station. I ask a hundred times, where is the station?

WOLF. Five minutes.

DORA. But where is the station?

MARCY. Five minutes.

DORA. But where is the station?

VOICES. (*Dispersedly.*) Five minutes, five minutes,
five minutes—

DORA. WHERE IS THE STATION?

(*Sudden SILENCE, faint BIRD SOUNDS made by the
actors, who have become a twisted WOODS.*)

DORA. Then I see a thick wood before me, which I
enter, and ask a man where the station is.

HERR K. Two hours more, two and a half hours, shall
I come along with you perhaps?

DORA. No, get away from me, I'll go alone, get away.

(*Eerie MUSIC BOX "Vienna Blood."*)

DORA. Then I see the station but I can't get to it, it's
like walking at the bottom of the ocean.

(MUSIC careening wildly into a grotesque backwards din.)

FATHER. ALL ABOARD.

(The NOISE abruptly stops.)

DORA. Then suddenly I'm home.

(Ticking CLOCK.)

DORA. I walk to the porter's lodge and ask for the key.
WOLF. *(As the porter, giving her a large key and making urgent but incomprehensible sounds.)* Uhhhhhhhhh. Uhhhhhhh. Uhhhhhhhh.
DORA. When I put the key in the lock, the maid opens the door.
MARCY. *(As the maid.)* Hello, miss. Ever such a nice day today, miss. Too bad they put your old dad in a box today, miss. So sad. We have violets. Snapdragons. Pussy willows. Sad.
DORA. Is Mother at home?
MARCY. They've all gone off to the cemetery, miss, every one.

(The PEOPLE sit in chairs like tombstones as DORA wanders among them, sound of WIND in the tombstones, made by the ACTORS whistling softly.)

MARCY. They're all there, good and bad, all gone. All lost and gone.
FREUD. Had you ever seen a town like this?

DORA. At Christmas a ridiculous young man I know sent me an album from a German health resort, with views of the town. I wanted to show it to someone the other day. Mother, where's the album Hans sent me?

MOTHER. (*Dusting the people in chairs.*) It's where you left it.

DORA. I left it right here.

MOTHER. Then it should be right here.

DORA. But it isn't right here.

MOTHER. Then it's someplace else.

DORA. Do you know where?

MOTHER. I might have put it in a box.

DORA. Why did you do that?

MOTHER. So I could put it away.

DORA. Why did you put it away?

MOTHER. Everything goes away sometime.

DORA. Where is the box?

MOTHER. It's gone.

FREUD. Who is this young man?

DORA. An engineer. He took a job in Germany so he could save some money. I think he might ask me to marry him. In Dresden he wanted to take me to the picture gallery but I went alone so I could stop as long as I wanted at the pictures I liked. I stayed two hours at the Sistine Madonna. (*SHE is looking through the window/picture frame at FRAU KLIPPSTEIN holding Peter.*) The dream was like Dresden.

FREUD. What pleased you so much about the Madonna?

DORA. I don't know.

FREUD. Pictures in an album, pictures in Dresden, the virgin mother, you search for a station, a box, a coffin, it contains a man, a woman contains a man in pregnancy, in the sexual act, you put the key in a lock, which is a container—

DORA. I asked Mother for a key, at a party last week.

(FRAU K hums the main waltz theme from "Tales from the Vienna Woods" and the tombstone people Mother has been dusting become PARTY GUESTS.)

MOTHER. So I said to her, I said, how can a woman live without doilies, and she said, Well, with little wet rings on the tables; but that's how they are, young girls have heads made of sawdust, they burn easily—

DORA. Mother, excuse me—

MOTHER. My little Dora, what a pretty little thing, but can she get a man? You'd think they'd be hanging around her like flies on cat poop, but Dora doesn't care.

DORA. Mother, where's the key to the cabinet?

MOTHER. When I was a girl at the dawn of time the days were made of twisted rhyme and the morning sang like morning doves but Dora doesn't care for love, she doesn't care at all.

DORA. Mother, please, Father wants some brandy, where's the key?

MOTHER. I tried to tell her, I said, Dora, soon you'll be fat and ugly and they'll snicker at you in the street, I said, do you think anybody cares about your soul? Who marries a nun?

DORA. Father can't sleep without his brandy.

MOTHER. When I was a girl my flesh would sing and the leaves were full of whispering and the young men died when they smelled my hair, but little Dora doesn't care, she doesn't care at all.

DORA. Where is the key? Please, where is the key?

MOTHER. This girl has a head like a cork.

DORA. MOTHER, I'VE ASKED YOU A HUNDRED TIMES, WHERE IS THE KEY?

(Silence. All the PEOPLE turn and look at Dora.)

MOTHER. I don't think you'll ever find it, dear.

HERR K. A toast: to Dora's father. Live many years in health.

FRAU K. To Dora's father. Many years.

DORA. I looked at my father's face and knew what he was thinking: he hadn't many years.

FREUD. What your father needed to get to sleep wasn't brandy, it was sexual release. He couldn't sleep because he couldn't have intercourse with the woman he loved. You craved revenge for this betrayal, so in your dream you left home and it killed him. Do you remember seeing a question mark inside a sentence like the note in the dream?

DORA. In the note Frau Klippstein wrote inviting me to the lake. And there are thick woods there, like the woods in the dream.

(The flute introduction to the zither section of "Tales from the Vienna Woods," measures 73-74, and MARCY appears as nymph as LIGHTS dim with the music.)

DORA. We were walking by those woods when Herr Klippstein attacked me. I ran away and asked a man how far it was back to our cabin. He said it was a two and a half hour walk, so I went back to the boat we'd come over on, and Herr Klippstein was there.

(The following three lines are simultaneous with the three annunciatory measures 75-77 which begin the zither section.)

HERR K. Dora, please—
DORA. Get away from me.
HERR K. Just five minutes—

(The PEOPLE have become WOODS again as the zither section begins, measures 78-89, and MARCY moves through them, curious and sad, pursued by WOLF, who can never quite manage to get close enough to touch her.)

DORA. The woods were like another picture I saw in Dresden, there were nymphs in it, scantily clad, running away.

(By the half note which concludes measure 89, MARCY is gazing out the window exactly where she was at the same point in the music in her second act entrance, and WOLF is just about to touch her when (90-93) SHE eludes him again up the steps to the bedroom, and HE follows as FREUD speaks over the last measures of the zither section (94-109).)

FREUD. The nymphae, as you may have gathered from Frau Klippstein's dirty books, is the name given to the labia minora, which lie in the background of the thick wood of the pubic hair. This is the fantasy that a man is trying to force his way into the female genitals.

(As the MUSIC moves to its climax MARCY lolls back on the bed invitingly, but when WOLF moves to throw himself upon her SHE slips away and on the last note HE has collapsed face down on the bed and SHE is gone.)

DORA. At the end of the dream I went upstairs and began reading a big book that lay open on a table. It was like Frau Klippstein's book, or the one I looked in when I was having stomach pains. And for a time after that I dragged my foot and avoided going up stairs.

FREUD. How long after the business at the lake was this?

DORA. Eight or nine months. Nine.

FREUD. So you had a pregnancy fantasy, and dragging your foot signified to the quite literal unconscious that you'd made, so to speak, a false step. You're still carrying around the burden of guilt for some secret we haven't found yet. What is it? What am I missing?

Scene 17

DORA. I don't think I have any more secrets. I think you've got secrets. Do you have secrets?

FREUD. Part of you wants me to find your secrets out, and will have great contempt for me if I don't. But another part of you hides them very skillfully.

DORA. I couldn't have contempt for you. You're the first person I've met who's almost as smart as I am, and I respect you for that. But not too much.

FREUD. Do you trust me?

DORA. Sometimes I trust you.

FREUD. Tell me a secret then.

DORA. I'll tell you one if you'll tell me one.

FREUD. All right. You first.

DORA. When I was a little girl, my room was right next to my parents, and some nights I could hear them breathing very hard and making the most extraordinary noises, like horses. I had nightmares about it.

FREUD. Was this about the time your asthma began?

DORA. You think I was trying to imitate them?

FREUD. Something like that.

DORA. Before my asthma, I was quite a wild little creature. I can still feel that little animal lurking inside me sometimes. Well, that's two secrets. Your turn.

FREUD. I'll tell you another time.

DORA. You owe me a secret. You promised.

FREUD. All right. My secret is that, despite all my investigations, one question continues to haunt me above all others. I haven't even come close to answering it, it torments me day and night, and that question is—

DORA. What does a woman want?

FREUD. How the hell did you know that?

DORA. Because I'm one smart cookie. You and I are both just too smart for our own good. We're doomed, we'll never be happy. And you have more secrets than that.

FREUD. Do I? Well, tell me, what secrets do I have? *(HE lays back on the couch, as patient.)*

DORA. (*Sitting in Freud's chair, playing with a cigar.*) You're ambitious, you want to be the best in the world. You're touchy, you have a special sense of your own dignity. You're honest, and sometimes you torture yourself over things you don't understand. You were probably a very romantic young man, but now that your wife is no longer beautiful, you've decided to pretend you were never like that. You look at young women in the street. You pretend that your interest in them is professional or fatherly, but you want them. Often when I'm upset you want to hold me and comfort me. Sometimes you want to kiss me and make love to me. And you will never admit this to anyone.

(*Towards the latter part of this FREUD has sat up, much more disconcerted by the possible truth in it than he would like her to see. HE starts to say something, hesitates, then, stonily:*)

FREUD. When did you first come to believe your father is impotent?

DORA. Pardon?

FREUD. You accused him of being impotent the day he nearly hit you. Did you mean that?

DORA. I don't know. Who cares? Was I right about your secret?

FREUD. Just answer the question.

DORA. No, you answer MY question.

FREUD. Dora, you project onto me feelings which—

DORA. I'm hungry. I want to quit.

FREUD. Here, have a lollipop. I keep them for children.

DORA. I'm not a child. Do I look like a child?

FREUD. Suit yourself.

DORA. All right. Give it here.

(SHE takes the lollipop and licks and sucks it through the following, an increasingly erotic process, while one by one in the background each of the MEN will light a cigar and each WOMAN try a lollipop.)

FREUD. If your father's impotent, how can he have an affair with Frau Klippstein?

DORA. There's more than one way to get sexual pleasure.

FREUD. Such as?

DORA. Oh, with the mouth, say. Oral stimulation of—various places. *(SHE starts to laugh, but it turns into a cough.)* You know, Doctor, if anybody believed a girl like me could even think such things, they'd see me as an incredibly perverted creature.

FREUD. Do you see yourself as a perverted creature?

DORA. No, I see YOU as a perverted creature, and me as your victim. *(SHE coughs again.)*

FREUD. You're coughing a great deal today.

DORA. I have a tickling in my throat.

FREUD. When you cough, you imagine yourself receiving sexual gratification.

DORA. Don't you ever cough?

FREUD. I have coughed, yes.

DORA. Maybe we could get together and cough some time.

FREUD. If we're ever sick together.

DORA. If people knew some of the things you and I talk about, they'd lock you up.

FREUD. I just follow where you lead me. I can't help you unless I understand, and I can't understand if I'm afraid to speak.

DORA. What if it came to a choice between helping me and understanding more? Which would you choose?

FREUD. I'd choose both.

DORA. What if you couldn't choose both?

FREUD. I'd choose both anyway.

DORA. If I told Father you and I talk about him and Frau Klippstein having oral sex, he'd say the sickness you see in me is a projection of the filth in your own soul. I think this transference is a two way street. You'd love to have me completely naked and helpless before you, wouldn't you? (*SHE sucks on the lollipop and lolls on the couch in an increasingly provocative manner.*)

FREUD. (*Getting very nervous.*) As a child, did you suck your thumb?

DORA. (*Playing with the buttons on her blouse.*) I remember sitting naked in the tub with Wolf and sucking for all I was worth—on my thumb, while pulling and yanking on his—earlobe. Disappointed?

FREUD. (*Pacing now and trying not to look at her as SHE begins unbuttoning her blouse.*) Many children clutch the nurse's earlobe while nursing. We get early gratification from sucking the nipple. When we transfer this sucking to the thumb, we may hold onto someone to keep the idea of connecting to another. And when the penis becomes the object of gratification, we combine the two and get pleasure from sucking the penis. So we see that this repulsive fantasy has a relatively innocent origin.

DORA. God, it's hot in here.

(FREUD turns and looks at DORA, who is stretching in an intensely erotic pose, and HE starts coughing. SHE points her finger at him, triumphant.)

DORA. GOT YOU. You coughed. And we all know what that means.

FREUD. (*Very flustered.*) I was simply clearing my throat.

DORA. (*Following him around the room, poking and tickling him, giggling at him, delighted at his embarrassment.*) Oh, no, there are no accidents. Naughty, naughty.

FREUD. Stop that. Are you all right?

DORA. (*Having a very good time chasing him.*) Oh, yes. I'm wonderful. Are you all right? What a funny man you are. I like you. You're not getting hot, are you? I'll open something.

FREUD. You're hysterical.

DORA. (*Poking him.*) No, YOU'RE hysterical. Poor little man, all his theories go right out the window when a real, live, flesh and blood girl touches him. Poor little thing, sucking on his cigar—

(SHE pokes him beneath the belt and FREUD slaps her once across the face—it is a practiced, professional slap for an hysteric, but HE is also clearly upset. SHE shuts up, astonished.)

DORA. You hit me.

FREUD. (*Going over to sit on the corner of his desk, his back away from her, composing himself.*) I may hit you again.

DORA. I doubt that very much.

(*SHE stomps over to Freud and pushes him very hard on the back with both hands. Off balance and off guard, HE flails his arms out and falls, face first, onto the floor, CRASH. Pause. DORA is sobered by his spectacular fall and a little worried that she has injured him.*)

FREUD. (*Sitting on the floor.*) Well, you win that round.

(*SHE reaches out to help him up, but HE avoids her hand, gets up on his own. DORA looks at him, then buries her face in his chest and holds him. FREUD doesn't know what to do. Finally HE touches her hair and her back, and holds her, comforting.*)

FREUD. Believe it or not, we're actually making very good progress. We're very close now.

DORA. I know we are.

FREUD. I mean to the truth.

DORA. Oh.

FREUD. Soon we'll find it, I think.

DORA. And then what?

FREUD. And then we'll be done.

DORA. And I'll never see you again.

FREUD. Yes.

DORA. (*Disengages and moves a little distance away from him.*) It doesn't matter. Today's the last time, anyway.

FREUD. The last time? Did you just decide that?

DORA. No. I made up my mind a couple of weeks ago that I'd probably just put up with you until the new year.

FREUD. So you gave me two weeks notice, only you didn't tell me.

DORA. I kept putting it off, like Marcy when she gave notice to the Klippsteins.

FREUD. Marcy gave notice to the Klippsteins? When?

(*HE looks across the stage at MARCY, who is getting dishes and cups to set the table.*)

DORA. At the lake.

FREUD. Before or after your encounter with Herr Klippstein?

DORA. The day before, I think. Why?

FREUD. Why did you never mention this?

DORA. I didn't think it was important. Since this is the last time, I think it's pointless for us to—

FREUD. If this is the last time then we must get as much done as we can. Now, why did she give notice?

DORA. I knew something was wrong from the extraordinary way she was behaving at breakfast.

Scene 18

(MARCY is setting the table, very upset, slamming chairs down, tossing dishes and silverware on the table. DORA watches with some alarm.)

DORA. Good morning, Marcy.
MARCY. (*Forced cheerfulness.*) Good morning.
DORA. Can I help you with that?
MARCY. No, I'll do it.

(SHE is stacking up a bizarre little pyramid of cup, saucer and silverware at Herr Klippstein's place. FRAU KLIPPSTEIN enters. MARCY abruptly storms into the kitchen.)

FRAU K. (*Watching Marcy go out.*) Good morning, Dora.
DORA. Good morning.
FRAU K. (*Looking at the table.*) Have the children been crawling on the table again?
DORA. Uh, no, actually—
HERR K. (*Breezing in.*) Good morning, my dear.
FRAU K. Good morning, dear.
HERR K. Good morning, Dora.
DORA. I hope so.

(MARCY comes storming back in, still seething, with a tray of breakfast—tea, toast, butter, marmalade.)

HERR K. Good morning, Marcy.

(SHE plunks the tray down and begins laying out things somewhat recklessly. HERR K observes the table setting.)

HERR K. Well, this looks good.

(FRAU K and DORA sit. HERR K sits. MARCY sits. HERR K is determined to be cheery.)

HERR K. Dear, could you please pass the toast?
FRAU K. Of course, dear. *(SHE does.)*
HERR K. Thank you.
FRAU K. You're welcome.
HERR K. Dora, could you pass the butter, please?
DORA. I don't see why not. *(SHE does.)*
HERR K. Thank you.
DORA. You're welcome.
HERR K. *(Buttering his toast.)* Marcy, could I please have some marmalade?

(MARCY turns away, getting apparently very interested in a spot on her skirt.)

HERR K. Marcy?
FRAU K. Marcy, could I please have some marmalade?
MARCY. Certainly. *(SHE passes it to Frau K.)*
FRAU K. Thank you, Marcy.
MARCY. Don't mention it.
FRAU K. *(Passing it to Herr K, not too pleasantly, then rising, smiling but grim.)* Excuse me. I believe I smell a rat. *(SHE goes up the steps to the bedroom.)*

HERR K. (*Standing and giving Marcy a murderous look.*) Excuse me. (*HE goes after his wife.*)

DORA. Marcy, what on earth is going on?

MARCY. Nothing. Everything is fine. I'm fine, he's fine, she's fine, everything's just ducky. Please leave me alone.

DORA. All right. (*SHE starts to go.*)

MARCY. Oh, God, don't you go, too. I don't want to be alone.

DORA. What is it?

MARCY. I'm not supposed to tell, but I can't help it. When Frau Klippstein was away in the country, Herr Klippstein made certain—advances towards me.

DORA. Did he?

MARCY. He made violent love to me and begged me to yield to him. He said he got nothing from his wife, and he was so very intense about it, he frightened me, and I didn't know what to do.

DORA. What DID you do?

MARCY. I said no, of course. (*SHE goes over to the window and looks out, as before.*) At first.

DORA. But eventually you gave in. And that's why you hate him.

MARCY. I don't know how I feel about him. He's polite to me when she's around, but the rest of the time he ignores me now, as if it never happened. I wrote and told my parents about it and they wrote back that I should leave the house right away. And when I didn't, they said they'd have nothing more to do with me, that I wasn't welcome at home any more.

DORA. Why didn't you leave when they told you to?

MARCY. I wanted to see if he might—change, somehow. I thought maybe he was just cold to me because he didn't want to hurt his wife. But I can't bear living like this. I'm giving my two weeks notice and going away.

DORA. Where are you going?

MARCY I don't know. Men are so horrible, Dora. It's awful, what they do to us, it's just hideous. I feel so small, like a postage stamp. I feel like some little bug. And I keep getting smaller and smaller.

FREUD. What happened to this girl?

DORA. She left. I don't know where she went. My brother tried to find out, but nobody seemed to know.

FREUD. Did she have a child as the result of this?

DORA. I don't know.

FREUD. This is the missing piece of the puzzle, Dora. Now I understand what happened between you and Herr Klippstein the next day.

DORA. I don't know what you mean.

FREUD. Yes you do.

Scene 19

(BIRD sounds. DORA walking with HERR K at the lake, exactly as in scene six.)

HERR K. You're such a pretty girl, Dora.

DORA. Yes, I know, but don't worry, I'll get over it.

HERR K. Have you got a boyfriend?

DORA. Don't be silly.

HERR K. I'm seldom silly.

DORA. I think boys my age should be killed.

HERR K. You'd prefer perhaps an older man.

DORA. I'd prefer nobody.

HERR K. The days can be lonely and terrible without someone to love. Also the nights.

DORA. I expect they can be equally lonely and terrible WITH someone to love.

HERR K. Ah, a woman of the world.

DORA. Don't make fun of me.

HERR K. I'd never do that. Would you like a cigarette?

DORA. No thank you.

HERR K. For most people the hope of love is all that keeps them going from one day to the next. One continues to hope for love, somehow, at some time, and one goes on. For people like us, that's all there is.

DORA. That's very sad.

HERR K. You're a wise girl after all, aren't you?

(HE reaches out his hand and touches her cheek, a gentle and sad gesture. SHE pulls away.)

HERR K. It's all right.

DORA. No, it's not all right.

HERR K. Are you afraid of me, Dora?

DORA. I'm not afraid of you, I'm disgusted by you.

HERR K. Am I so despicable because I'm lonely? Because I enjoy your company and sometimes I can't help wanting to touch you? I live in a prison, Dora, there are beautiful things passing by out the windows but I can't touch them, it's horrible, I get no tenderness, I get no comfort, I feel such a desperate need for some kind of warmth, Dora, I need you to be my friend. Don't turn me away.

DORA. You've got your wife to be your friend.

HERR K. I get nothing from my wife, Dora, please, could I just—

(HE moves towards her and SHE hits him very hard across the face.)

DORA. You got something from Marcy, though, didn't you?

HERR K. From Marcy? What do you mean?

DORA. My God, can't you even change your speech a bit from one victim to the next?

HERR K. What kind of stories has she been telling you? The girl isn't well, Dora, she imagines things, she's overly interested in sexual matters, I saw her reading filthy books with my wife, she—

DORA. Get away from me.

HERR K. Dora, please, listen, when a man is desperate—

DORA. GET AWAY OR I'LL SCREAM.

HERR K. She goes around in her nightgown when my wife's away, she leaves the door to her room open—Dora, what is a man supposed to do when his wife won't let him touch her and a young girl offers herself to him? We're only flesh and blood, have some compassion for us, you'll need it for yourself soon enough. AT LEAST I'M ALIVE, AT LEAST I CAN TOUCH OTHER HUMAN BEINGS. THAT SEEMS TO BE MORE THAN YOU'RE CAPABLE OF. (*SHE has run away, back to Freud.*) WE'RE ONLY FLESH AND BLOOD.

FREUD. That's why you were so angry at him. It wasn't that his suggestions offended you, but that he'd said the same thing in the same words to Marcy earlier. It was jealousy.

DORA. I'd have reacted the same way if I hadn't known about Marcy.

FREUD. I don't think so. Look how deeply you've identified yourself with her in your dream and your conduct. When did you tell your father what happened at the lake? Right away?

DORA. A couple of weeks later.

FREUD. You gave Herr Klippstein two weeks for the same reason Marcy didn't leave immediately, because she still had hopes, and so did you. You were waiting to see if he'd repeat his proposals. If he had, you might have given in.

DORA. I had no intention of giving in.

FREUD. Did he contact you after the lake?

DORA. He sent me one postcard. Then nothing.

FREUD. So you got revenge by telling your father. Maybe you thought accusing him would somehow bring him back to see you.

DORA. He offered to come, but he never did. But I don't see what good it would have done.

FREUD. The Klippsteins had spoken of divorce, hadn't they? Did you think he might want to divorce her and marry you?

DORA. I was only sixteen.

FREUD. How old was your mother when she married your father?

DORA. Sixteen. But I don't think marriage is what he had in mind.

FREUD. (*Excited and increasingly triumphant.*) But you didn't let him finish. How do you know what he might have said? Perhaps a divorce might have resulted, your father getting Frau Klippstein and you getting her husband. You must have been horribly disillusioned when he responded by slandering you to your father. Nothing makes you so angry as the assertion that you imagined the incident at the lake. What you DID imagine was that Herr Klippstein wouldn't leave off until he married you. That's why it hurt you so much when it didn't happen and why you had the dreams and symptoms of pregnancy nine months later. In short, we have proven your deep love for Herr Klippstein, which is exactly what you challenged me to prove.

DORA. All right. You're right. I concede, I admit it, I loved Herr Klippstein, I wanted him to make love to me and I wanted to marry him. Now will you just leave me alone?

FREUD. You admit this freely?

DORA. Yes, I admit it, you're right about everything.

FREUD. You sincerely mean this? You're not just trying to make me happy?

DORA. I don't want to make you happy, I just want you to leave me alone.

(FREUD is troubled. HE looks at each of the other people in turn, thinking, scratching his head.)

DORA. What's the matter? I thought you'd be pleased. I've just admitted what you want. You've won, you've now seen me in entire nakedness. So we're done.

FREUD. (*His gaze coming to rest, finally, on Frau K.*) Something's not right. You agree too easily.

DORA. We've been fighting for months, now I admit you're right and you're still not happy? What do you want from me?

FREUD. There's one thing deeper yet, and you've just allowed my vanity this little triumph to keep me from getting to it.

DORA. There isn't anything deeper.

FREUD. (*Looking at Frau Klippstein.*) There's another way, you know, to interpret your intense jealousy over the relations between your father and Frau Klippstein.

DORA. And what's that?

FREUD. Did you have intense friendships in your early teen years? Did you hold hands with your girl friends and kiss them and swear undying devotion to one another?

DORA. That's what girls do.

FREUD. Some girls do more.

DORA. What are you getting at?

FREUD. When you stayed with the Klippsteins, who did you sleep with?

DORA. Frau Klippstein.

FREUD. In the summer did you sleep naked together?

DORA. No, we wore raccoon coats, what kind of question is that?

FREUD. You discussed sex with her more than once, didn't you? Herr Klippstein wasn't lying about that, was he? Answer me.

(*DORA makes her way slowly up the steps to the bedroom, her eyes all the while on FRAU KLIPPSTEIN, who has been waiting for her, sitting on the edge of the bed.*)

Scene 20

(DORA and FRAU KLIPPSTEIN sit on the bed, watching the sunset, bathed in reddish LIGHT.)

FRAU K. Your father is such a nice man, Dora. Not like my husband. My husband is such a brute. Most men are monsters in bed. Your father is such a gentle man. I imagine he is.

DORA. Tell me what it's like.

FRAU K. I can't tell you how it feels. I can't describe it. It's indescribable.

DORA. Is it very horrible?

FRAU K. At first it seems a little horrible. At least, it did to me. But one gets used to it, and then one starts to like it, and before long one simply can't do without it.

DORA. Is one allowed to enjoy it?

FRAU K. Well, who's to stop one?

DORA. I wish I knew how it feels.

FRAU K. Have you never—not, of course, but I mean—not even—

DORA. I'm frightened to death of it. Of everything about it.

FRAU K. Don't be frightened. There's nothing to be frightened of.

DORA. Yes there is.

FRAU K. No, believe me, there's nothing to be frightened of, if you just relax. Relax. Just relax. Trust me. *(SHE touches Dora's hair.)*

FREUD. She betrayed you, didn't she?

DORA. No. What do you mean?

FREUD. You loved her and she betrayed you to your enemies, to the men, she told her husband you were a wicked girl who read filthy books. She only cared about you as a way of getting to your father. You were jealous of your father and Frau Klippstein because you wanted her for yourself. Your love for her husband was an attempt to make her jealous, to replace her, to become her, to become the beloved.

DORA. That's filth, that's horrible filth.

FREUD. Your resentment against the men in your life was in direct proportion to your desire for this woman they all wanted and that everyone seemed to possess but you. So part of you loved your father and he betrayed you with Frau Klippstein, and part of you loved Herr Klippstein and he betrayed you with his wife and with Marcy, and your deepest love was for Frau Klippstein, and she betrayed you with everybody. All the people you loved betrayed you and the one you loved most deeply and most secretly betrayed you most of all, and in your grief and outrage you struck back at all of them.

DORA. THAT ISN'T TRUE, IT ISN'T TRUE, IT ISN'T TRUE.

(SHE is crying and trying to get away, but FREUD won't let her go, HE holds her arms and makes her look at him.)

DORA. LET ME GO. GET YOUR HANDS OFF ME.

FREUD. Look at me. LOOK AT ME. I have no more use for your truths. My truth is superior to your truth because my truth WORKS, my truth will make you free, my truth is freedom, yours is slavery. Accept my truth and be well.

DORA. BUT I KNOW IT ISN'T TRUE.

FREUD. You wish to be unhappy?

DORA. NO.

FREUD. You wish to keep on being sick?

DORA. NO.

FREUD. You love your illness, you worship it, it comforts you, you protect it ingeniously, but your intelligence is a curse to you if you only use it to keep yourself sick.

DORA. You prefer stupid women.

FREUD. I prefer FREE women.

DORA. But if I was free I wouldn't need you.

FREUD. That's perfectly true.

DORA. Then you want to get rid of me, you're just like them, you don't care about me, either.

FREUD. I'm trying to give you the tools to heal yourself with, but you must do the healing yourself, nobody can do it for you.

DORA. (*Pulling away.*) I'm getting out of here.

FREUD. You do and you reject truth, you reject happiness, you reject life—

DORA. (*Turning back on him.*) No I don't. I reject YOU.

FREUD. As long as you're the victim of these destructive passions and self-deceptions and as long as you fail to admit their true origins, you have no control over your life, and you live among lies.

DORA. How can a man understand a woman? How can anybody be so arrogant as to think he can understand another person so completely? If I don't understand why I do what I do, how can YOU hope to? Sometimes it feels like you're MY patient and I'm trying to make YOU sane. It's like we're having a war over who's sane and who's not.

FREUD. Lose the war. Be sane.

DORA. Why do you have to keep torturing me like this?

FREUD. There is no growth without pain. I know this, I've had these wars with myself.

DORA. Did you win or lose? I think the insane Dr. Freud won over the sane one and is now impersonating him so he can torment me. You hate me, don't you?

FREUD. I don't hate you. I'm much too fond of you, and you know it, but I must use this fondness to help you, it must never get in the way.

DORA. But you're so cruel to me.

FREUD. When I need to be.

DORA. You play God.

FREUD. When it's necessary.

DORA. Isn't it just possible, just remotely possible that even though you're so smart and experienced and older and a man, isn't it still possible that I'm right and you're wrong?

FREUD. I don't dispute your logic, but I find the consequences at best useless and at worst destructive, and I suspect your motives.

DORA. Then we're even.

FREUD. Dora, there's a whole adult world out there for you to enter.

DORA. But I don't want it. Their world is horrible, they grasp at whatever sordid relief they can get, they use each other disgracefully, they betray so easily, they move from one partner to another like putting on a new suit. I do not wish to play this hideous game with them.

(Pause.)

FREUD. Sometimes if we're very clever we understand things too soon, and then we think we've understood everything, and we stop looking.

DORA. Yes, that's very clever, but I have a response to that which I think you'll find utterly unanswerable.

FREUD. And what is that?

DORA. I'm leaving, and I'm never coming back. *(SHE runs out.)*

FREUD. Dora—*(HE stands there. HE takes off his spectacles and rubs his eyes. Then HE sits down at his desk and holds his forehead with both his hands.)*

Scene 21

(FATHER comes over to Freud's desk, smoking his cigar.)

FATHER. So, how am I? Are you listening?

FREUD. You're much better.

FATHER. I feel much better.

FREUD. Good.

FATHER. Aren't you going to ask me how my daughter is?

FREUD. How is your daughter?

FATHER. I think she wants to come and see you again, but pride or something—it's hard for her to admit that she's been imagining all those things. She thinks you believe her story about Herr Klippstein.

FREUD. Of course I believe it. So do you. I must tell you frankly that I think Dora was correct in her assessment of many things in her life, including her belief that you supported this treatment because you expected me to convince her that your affair with Frau Klippstein was imaginary. She doesn't trust me any more, and I'm not sure I blame her.

FATHER. That isn't my fault.

FREUD. I didn't say it was.

FATHER. I thought things were going well.

FREUD. They were going TOO well. Leaving was partly an act of vengeance against me for discovering her secrets. What I discovered hurt her, and she had to hurt me in return.

FATHER. You sound as if she actually DID hurt you.

FREUD. No one who summons up demons in the breast of another can expect to survive without scars. When one wrestles with demons, one is bloodied. I had become dangerous, I knew too much, and she had to reject me. The physician is helpless in this respect, she can take out all her resentment on him, and punish him by removing herself from his life. And so she did.

FATHER. Are you saying a cure is impossible?

FREUD. Sometimes deeply felt emotion can knock down barriers—anger, love. And sometimes the doctor must be removed before the patient can get better.

FATHER. So where do we go from here?

FREUD. I'll send you a bill.

Scene 22

(BIRD sounds. FREUD opens the window seat, gets gloves and plants in a wooden tray, gets down on his knees and begins to putter around in his garden. DORA appears behind him, dressed in black, looking especially grown up and lovely. SHE watches him for a moment, amused to see him in such a position, and finally works up the courage to speak.)

DORA. Dr. Freud?

FREUD. (*Not looking around, cranky.*) Yes? What is it?

DORA. Anna said I'd find you out here.

FREUD. I'm sorry, but I told that girl—(*HE sees who it is.*) Dora? My goodness, how are you? (*HE gets up, goes to shake hands, realizes he's holding out a dirty glove.*) I'm all dirty. I've been digging in the garden, an exceedingly stupid thing for a man like me to try, I have no talent for it and no hope of acquiring any, but I felt an urge, I don't know why, I will no doubt give it up, and no one will ever know about it, so you mustn't tell—(*HE sees that SHE is smiling at him.*) I'm babbling, aren't I?

DORA. I like it. I've never seen you babble, it's cute. And you're not so godlike.

FREUD. Perhaps gardening and babble go together. God planted a garden, didn't he? And look how that turned out. The garden of babble. You look wonderful.

DORA. So do you.

FREUD. I look old. But you're lovely, you're really—I haven't seen you in so long.

DORA. It's April first. Fifteen months.

FREUD. Well, how are you?

DORA. I'm all right. I think I'm all right. But I'd like to talk to you.

FREUD. Of course. Would you like to go inside?

DORA. No, I like it better out here. You don't babble in your office. I feel more evenly matched.

FREUD. All right.

DORA. For some weeks after I left you I was very confused and unhappy, but then gradually I began to feel better, and my attacks happened less frequently. Then last May one of the Klippstein children died, and I decided to pay a sympathy call.

(In the bedroom, MARCY in mourning, with the dead doll-child PETER in her arms. On the sofa, the KLIPPSTEINS, also in mourning.)

FRAU K. We haven't seen you in such a long time, Dora. I hope you've been well.

DORA. I've been worse.

FRAU K. We've missed you. I've missed you. Haven't you missed Dora, dear?

HERR K. Yes, I've missed her, too.

FRAU K. I thought you had. You must say hello to Marcy, Dora. She's come back for the funeral. And tell your brother. Grindl was so happy to see her. My son loved her, too. He drowned, you know. Perhaps if she'd never had to leave—(*SHE looks at Herr K, then away.*)

DORA. There's something I need to talk to you about. I've thought about this a great deal, and I don't mean to upset you in your time of sorrow, but perhaps this is the best time for us to talk about this—it's harder to lie when someone has died, and so much in our lives has been left unsaid, I thought that now one might just come out and say what one actually thinks, or at least what one thinks one thinks—I mean, what one really feels, behind all the lies and the politeness and—

FRAU K. Is this really something we should be discussing now?

DORA. I know you've had an affair with my father.

(The KLIPPSTEINS look at each other. FRAU KLIPPSTEIN seems to be asking HERR KLIPPSTEIN for help, but HE looks away.)

DORA. This is your business and not mine, but I need to have just one admission from your husband. I want him to admit that what happened at the lake that day wasn't just my imagination.

FRAU K. I fail to see what purpose there is in raking up all this pain again.

DORA. Just so I can hear it from him, it's important to me. Please.

FRAU K. I think it would be better if you left now.

DORA. But how could you let them all think I was crazy, or a liar, or some sort of sex-crazed, awful—

FRAU K. Dora, I must insist, really—

DORA. Both of you, how COULD you?

FRAU K. Dora—

DORA. Would you lie over the dead body of your child?

FRAU K. I forbid you to upset my husband like this. Leave him alone. You can say what you want about me, but just let him alone, you have no right to—

HERR K. I was lonely.

FRAU K. You don't have to say a thing.

HERR K. I thought if I denied everything that you, being an innocent girl, would come in time to believe my version of it and forget your own. I misjudged you. There is no excuse. Forgive me. Please forgive me if you can.

FRAU K. Is that what you wanted to hear?

DORA. I don't know. I didn't mean to upset you.

FRAU K. My husband and I have come to an understanding about these matters recently.

(The KLIPPSTEINS hold hands.)

DORA. That's very nice. I should go now.

FRAU K. Come and see us again some time, won't you? You must. You really must. *(FRAU K smiles at her, a sad but genuinely affectionate smile.)*

DORA. *(To Freud.)* I went right home and told my father.

FATHER. Dora, I wish you wouldn't run off like that without telling us where you're going. Your mother worries about you.

DORA. Why are you always hiding behind Mother? If you're worried about me, say so. It isn't a crime. I went to give my sympathy to the Klippsteins. Herr Klippstein confessed. In front of his wife he confessed that he made improper advances towards me at the lake, and that he lied about it afterwards.

FATHER. Did he? I should go over there immediately and thrash the man, if it weren't for the death of his child, and the pain it would give to his wife.

DORA. You knew he was lying. I also told Frau Klippstein I knew about her affair with you, in front of her husband.

FATHER. And did she confess that, too?

DORA. She didn't deny it.

FATHER. This sounds like quite a confessional. You should have brought in a priest.

DORA. I don't tell you this to give you pain, or to win some kind of game with you, but to show you that I'm not sick, and if I WAS sick, it's because I caught it from you people.

FATHER. What you call sickness is simply life.

DORA. Then why did you blame me for wanting to die? It seems like the only cure for it.

FATHER. No, you mustn't believe that, no matter what you think of us, there is still hope for you, even in the midst of all this humiliation and betrayal, there are moments of integrity, fragments of beauty. You must learn to find them, like the rest of us. You're an adult now.

DORA. But I wasn't an adult THEN. You were supposed to help me, not use me.

FATHER. I did the best I could.

DORA. Well, it wasn't enough. It wasn't nearly enough.

(HE looks at her, seems much older now, turns and goes sadly upstage towards Mother, but stops before he gets to her.)

Scene 23

(Calliope waltz, eerie, "Vienna Blood," as in scene fourteen. As this scene progresses, WOLF and MARCY meet at the carnival and talk shyly with one another.)

DORA. Then in October there was the street carnival again, and I was walking home through the crowd and remembering the day in Herr Klippstein's office, when suddenly there he was, on the corner in front of me.

(HERR K has seen her. THEY look at each other from across the stage.)

DORA. He looked so sad and so much older there in the street, I felt something—it wasn't like what I'd felt for him before—

(HERR K turns and starts to go.)

DORA. Wait. Don't go.

(HE stops, uncomfortable.)

DORA. How are you?
HERR K. I'm the same.
DORA. And how is your wife?
HERR K. She's the same, too. She speaks of you often.
DORA. Does she? What does she say about me?
HERR K. That she misses you.
DORA. I don't think she does.

HERR K. She does. It's true.

(Pause. Just the MUSIC. MARCY turns and walks away from WOLF, who is left standing there.)

DORA. We've made it at last to the carnival.
HERR K. Unfortunately, much too late.
DORA. *(To Freud.)* I looked at him and it seemed, to my astonishment, that he was going to cry.
HERR K. I have business, excuse me—
DORA. No, wait—

(HE rushes away, half looking back at her, confused and embarrassed. The MUSIC gets louder and speeds up insanely.)

DORA. NO, LOOK OUT, LOOK OUT.

(The MUSIC stops suddenly, and so does HERR K, upstage, with his back to her.)

DORA. He was looking back at me and he stepped right in the path of a carriage. He was hurt rather badly, but he's nearly recovered now. His wife nurses him. She's still good at that. At least she's somehow connected to life, to people and flesh. As I am not.

(Pause. FREUD looks at her.)

DORA. I'm all right now, though. I have a job, in an office, and I'm much absorbed in my work. I'm good at it, too. I think one's work is very important, maybe it's the only important thing—even Mother's work, dusting the house over and over, is at least some action to get deeply involved in.

FREUD. What about your young man in Germany?

DORA. We write letters. He's a foolish boy, still full of romantic love and nonsense like that. I think romantic love is the unfortunate union of lust and neurosis, don't you?

FREUD. I don't think I'd put it quite that way.

DORA. A couple of weeks ago I saw an article about you in the paper, and since then I've had neuralgia on one side of my face. You taught me about the connections between such things, and I thought I should come and ask you about it.

FREUD. You feel guilty about Herr Klippstein's accident, and you remember slapping his face at the lake. Seeing the article led you to think about this the way I would. You've no doubt already figured that out.

DORA. Yes, you've made me terribly clever.

FREUD. You were terribly clever long before you met me.

DORA. But I hadn't anyone else who was also terribly clever. That makes an enormous difference. Look, I just want you to understand that although I can't accept all your conclusions, I think you were right about many things, and I want to thank you for helping me cure myself.

FREUD. Dora—

DORA. Oh, dear, it's getting late, I've got to go.

FREUD. Dora, forgive me, but if you think you're cured, you're still deluding yourself.

DORA. What an awful thing to say, after I've come to see you and everything. Don't spoil things now.

FREUD. I can't help it, I must tell you the truth, the strongest current in your unconscious life remains your love for Frau Klippstein. The deepest repression, the core of your problem, is still unresolved. You spent most of your time with me trying often quite brilliantly to direct my attention away from this, you're doing it now, you use my loneliness and fondness for you to—

DORA. You will NEVER understand women, you will NEVER, NEVER understand them. I don't think any man ever will, but the slimy ones like my father and Herr Klippstein understand them in their own way much better than hypocrites like you ever can.

FREUD. (*Putting his hand on her shoulder.*) Dora, listen—

DORA. (*Pulling away violently.*) Get away from me. Don't touch me.

(THEY stand at a little distance from each other, both miserable.)

DORA. Maybe I'll go to Germany and marry my idiotic young man. I hope that will be proof enough for you. I'll be sane just to spite you.

FREUD. You don't have to prove anything to me, just find some way to accept these people for who they are— not to excuse them or condone what they did to you but to acknowledge your feelings for them so you can forgive them and get on with your life.

DORA. They don't deserve to be forgiven.

FREUD. It's not for their sake, it's for yours. What you can't forgive will enslave you forever.

DORA. And what about you? Am I supposed to forgive you, too?

FREUD. Whatever I've done, whether I was right or wrong, all I meant to do was reduce the amount of suffering I found. I hope you understand that.

DORA. Be careful, Doctor, that you don't think yourself into useless realities you can't extricate yourself from. That's what madness is, you taught me that. Your truth is no longer useful to me, so I'm throwing it away, you taught me that, too. Look for my marriage announcement in the papers. I'd send you an invitation, but I know how busy you are with all those unhappy people. I'm sure you'll never come to the end of them.

HE hesitates, moves towards him slightly, then checks herself, turns and walks upstage, stopping with her back him as the introduction to the main waltz theme of 'Emperor Waltz" is heard—the end of measure 53, REUD begins sadly to put his gloves and plants 'o the windowseat. FATHER approaches Dora asks her to dance. SHE looks at him, looks 'EUD, who has his back to them through all Father, moving cautiously towards him, d, lets him place his other hand on her 'ck at Freud once more, and as the main gins (measure 76) DORA and her hesitantly at first, to dance. At 'owing confidence, SHE is snatched 'ance this faster sequence, and 'sk Mother to dance. At measures aches and asks her to dance, and 'y as (110-125) DORA dances with HERR K and FATHER and MOTHER dance. Then DORA leaves Herr K at Frau K, looks at her a moment, then turns to look back at FREUD, still alone downstage with his back to them, looking out the window, and SHE moves downstage towards Freud as FATHER and MOTHER, WOLF and MARCY dance and HERR K approaches Frau K (126-133). DORA touches Freud's shoulder and HE turns to her (134). SHE offers to dance with him as HERR and FRAU K begin dancing with the OTHERS (135-141). Here edit back to measure 92 as FREUD and DORA dance with the OTHER THREE COUPLES (92-106), then a second edit, all the way to the very last 21 measures of "The Emperor," as the PEOPLE move into the formal group pose that signals the FLASH and CLICK that signify the last photograph, which should be taken at the final notes of the music, the climax of the waltz. BLACKOUT.)

NOTES

1 (Genesis)

In October of 1900, when the patient Freud was to call Dora in his account of the case walked into his office, Freud was nothing like the worshipped and vilified demonic twentieth century god he was to become later in his life and especially after his death. He was forty-four years old, and was to live another thirty-nine years. Of the series of great books upon which his fame was to rest, only *The Interpretation of Dreams* had been published, less than a year earlier, and it had dropped quietly into a sea of indifference. He had been married fourteen years and had a house full of children to support. He was younger, more vulnerable, and more troubled by his failure to make much of a splash in the world than either his worshippers or his detractors generally like to picture him.

When I read Freud's account of his treatment of Dora, it seemed to me unlike his other writings in some way that I could not immediately identify. There was something not right about it. In his other books, which I had been reading with pleasure since I was fourteen, I had found him to be a powerful, precise and entertaining writer with a surprising sense of humor and a scrupulous passion for accuracy. Whatever I might think of the conclusions he reached—and many of them seemed to me even more bizarre than the behavior they attempted to explain—I had always respected his courage in following his investigations wherever they led him, and in drawing the conclusions they led him to, no matter how shocking or utterly grotesque they might seem. I discovered early on that one did not have to agree with Freud to learn from him and be entertained by him, and that Freud was a much more accomplished writer than most of his disciples, even Jung, whose even more bizarre works were to intrigue me later. But Freud's account of Dora seemed different—it was not just that it was so early in the body of his work—it was that he seemed, very uncharacteristically, to be holding something back, to be avoiding an issue which seemed to lurk in the text but was hardly dealt with there—his own growing emotional involvement with his patient. I have no proof to offer for this. I am not an expert on Freud and am by nature neither a disciple nor a believer. My instincts told me something, and I wrote a play to find out if it was true. Of course, a play never decides what is true or false, it merely allows the playwright to share his delusions with congregations of others. Freud dealt with the world his way, I deal with the world mine. I wrote a play.

2 (Writing)

This is how it is for me—it is no doubt different for others. There is a voice. It does not always speak. But when it speaks, if you're a writer, you've got to listen and get it down. Don't ask questions, not then. Don't stop to polish. Get it down while the voice is speaking. Pay attention to the goddess while she is present. For when she is gone, you can't summon her up again at will. If you put it off, you will forget. She will be silent. You cannot force her to come. Later, when she is silent, you can worry about the cutting, condensing, applying the craft you have learned to what you have written down. You use the rational part of your brain to do rewrites. You use the other part, pre-rational, unpredictable, primitive and strange, to generate what you write. Or rather, it uses you, and if you are smart, you let it. And if you do this for years and are loyal to the goddess, she will help you by whispering now and then during the rewrites and by letting the rational part of your brain watch respectfully when she is in her transmitting mode. This is how it feels. That's all I can say about it.

3 (The Dance of Life)

There is a painting by Edvard Munch called "The Dance of Life," completed in 1900, the year of Freud and Dora. In this painting we see a young girl in a white dress, looking on among dancers at another image of herself in a red dress, dancing with a somewhat lecherous looking man. In the background, other young girls in white dance with other young men—one young man looks like a vampire, about to sink his teeth into the neck of his partner. And on the other side of the picture, the same girl looks sadly back at herself dancing, only now she is alone again, dressed in black. In white her hands are open, anxious to touch. In red, as she is dancing, her one hand is locked about the young man's neck, her other hand clutched in his at the level at which their genitals touch, and in black her hands are clutched together before her. It is a sad picture—the dance is presented as both impossibly enticing and yet inevitably tragic. She is innocent, a bit frightened, but filled with desire for the contact of the dance. Then she is dancing, and the dance goes by in a kind of hot nightmare of unreality, and then she is alone again, looking back on her former self, all hope lost. And yet it is also a beautiful painting, with the beauty of tragedy. This is the dance Dora wants to participate in, but also fears and mistrusts, and for good reasons. And yet there is only the dance. There is really nothing else.

4 (Freud as Detective)

He spends the play trying to solve a mystery, to put together the living pieces of a complex puzzle, and he must not, in production, be stuck behind his desk. Like each of the other characters, he must be free to explore at one time or another every part of the set in his quest for the truth— he watches the scenes progress, moves about to investigate, to get a better view—he is not a stationary voice behind a desk, he is much more like Sherlock Holmes in the heat of an investigation. His mind is active, one of the most attractive things about him is that we can see him thinking, figuring, excited, troubled, trying out answers, screwing up, missing things we can see, then brilliantly finding things we didn't see and showing us they were there all along. Whether he succeeds or fails, whether we ultimately agree or disagree with his conclusions, he must take us along with him in his investigation if the play is to work properly, and we must be engaged by his fascination with Dora and with the elegantly tangled labyrinth of her world. He is our guide. We may not always trust him, but we must like him enough to follow him, despite the enormous bag of preconceptions we have probably brought in with us. All guides are ultimately suspect, because we must ultimately make our own discoveries and draw our own conclusions. That doesn't mean they're bad guides. It just means that we must not forget that they are neither gods nor demons. They are only human, like us. Lies are complex, but so is truth.

5 (Names)

Heinrich and Elsa Murnau and their children Wolf and Dora. Rudy and Anna Klippstein and their children Peter and Grindl. Marcy Kleiner. Freud contributed the name Dora and the initial K for the family she is obsessed with. I made up the rest. All of these people actually existed, had different names, played out their own plays. The doll children should be simple stuffed creatures with joints at knees and elbows, dressed in modest period clothing, with no faces except for Victorian button eyes. They must be handled by the actors carefully and with love, treated in all cases as real children, and should be tended in the course of the play mostly by Marcy, whose relationship with them is extremely close. Mother loves to baby sit them. Herr K adores them and we should see that he is a good father much of the time. Frau K is a little afraid of them—she is jealous of their love for Marcy, but has no real idea how to relate to them. Wolf is their great friend, and spends much time with them and Marcy. Dora loves them and spends as much time with them as her busy agenda in this play will allow. Father also plays with them, and even Freud will keep friendly company with them while he is watching Dora and listening. The children, like the other actors, will in the course of the play go everywhere onstage, all times and places, as always, interpenetrating and coexisting simultaneously.

As I have made up names, I have also invented certain events and relationships, but almost everything in this play has some very recognizable referent in Freud's account of the case, which I very much recommend, both for what it says, which is fascinating, and for what it doesn't say, which is ultimately what the play came to be about. Note especially Philip Rieff's brilliant introduction to the Collier Books edition.

6 (Dates)

1882 Dora born in Vienna.

1888 Dora is six. Her family meets the Klippsteins at a health resort.

1896 Dora is fourteen.   In October, she is first approached by Herr K in the carnival office scene.

1898 Summer. The events at the lake. Dora is sixteen.

1900 October. Dora begins analysis with Freud. She is eighteen.

    31 December. Dora ends analysis.

1901 May. Death of Peter Klippstein.

1902 April 1. Dora returns to see Freud for the last time.

1903 Dora is married. She is twenty-one.

1905 Freud publishes Dora's case, which he had written immediately after the analysis ended.

7 (Anachronism)

Every play is a great moving anachronistic flesh and blood mechanism, a thing out of its proper time and place, a set of conventions played out in the present, representing the past, altering the future. No doubt Freud would not have written on his little pad that Dora was one smart cookie. But what he might have written, in German, was an equivalent idiomatic expression current among German speaking people in Vienna around 1900. I have no idea what this would have been, but I don't think its most useful English translation would be "This young woman is extremely intelligent." Each play creates its own universe of discourse and its own dramatic grammar, and what matters is to capture in language the emotional sense of how people are relating to each other when they use words. Persons raised on American Realism sometimes find it difficult to understand the difference between Realism, which is simply a set of dramatic conventions, and Reality, which is the sum of all possible conventions. Those persons most disturbed by what they consider to be anachronisms in my plays have not read Shakespeare very carefully. Anyone who had read Plutarch closely enough to crib plays from him must also have observed that the ancient Romans were not in the habit of blowing each other away with firearms. Shakespeare, a very practical fellow and a theatre person of some experience, understood that any play is merely a set of conventions and that no particular set of conventions is in itself either more or less real than any other. What happens on a stage is an archetypal focus of all times and places, past, present and future. It is in the theatre that we experience the illusion of freeing ourselves from the tyranny of time by observing a set of actions which is at once a thing in and out of time. Every play makes its own truth, and if its magic be compelling enough, the audience, reluctantly or not, will learn, in the course of time, to adjust. If the playwright is lucky, this will happen some time before he is dead.

8 (Playing Without The Ball)

As much of the texture of this play in performance comes from the presence of most of the players most of the time, a great deal of care in rehearsals must be devoted to the nonverbal activities of characters not directly involved in any given scene. The best way to do this is to call the whole cast to most rehearsals, and to encourage actors without lines in a given scene to relate to each scene and each of the other characters in a very direct way as the spoken scenes are being rehearsed. Everyone is, in effect, in virtually every moment of every scene. This interpenetration of every character into every scene may in the early rehearsals look rather like a fire drill in a mental ward, but it is necessary to establish from the beginning the close web of emotional and symbolic interconnections that bind each of the characters to each of the others across time and space in this very interconnected little universe— this is not something that can be stuck in later after the spoken parts of the scenes have been blocked. It must all grow organically together through the rehearsal period or it won't work. The actors will, given the proper freedom and encouragement, generally find many more moments of interpenetration than can ultimately be used, and as rehearsals progress it will be the director's job to tell them what to keep, and to help them gradually pare away the rest. The play should come to resemble a kind of elaborate dance with many moving parts constantly shifting in time and space. Actors not directly involved in a given scene must be especially sensitive to when their characters are being talked about, and when something or somebody they care deeply about is being discussed. Each actor should thus in the course of rehearsals create an ongoing relationship between his character and each of the others both in and out of the spoken scenes. Wolf and Marcy, who have the least to say, have nevertheless just as much acting to do, and a rather complex story to tell, which works as a direct or ironic counterpoint to Dora's adventures throughout the play, involving their innocent meetings with the children, growing affection, an estrangement evident at the beginning of the second act resulting from Marcy's experience with Herr K—the audience, of course, sees the effect here before they know the cause, an important motif in this play—their avoidance of each other, and, after Marcy's return for the funeral, and a second encounter at the carnival, their final coming together in the last dance. In a like manner each of the other couples goes through an evolving emotional relation in the course of the play, and much of this must be discovered gradually by the actors as they move through rehearsals. When this play is being approached properly, there should be no moment in rehearsal when any actor is merely waiting around to come on, and no moment in performance in which any character is not actively involved onstage, except for those few moments in which now and then actors must disappear briefly for costume changes. There are no empty spaces, there are no blackouts except where indicated, the transitions are fluid and usually instantaneous—we never have to wait for actors to come on or get into place because the actors are already there. The way the play moves is always a part of the play.

9 (Theatre And The Unconscious)

In order to be set in motion, a dream needs both an instigator and a source of energy. What happens to the conscious self during the day acts as the instigator. What sets it off in your unconscious, a buried wish that is somehow touched by this instigation, is the source of energy. The same process is the process of creation when one writes or paints. There is an external stimulus, often apparently arbitrary and perhaps unremarkable to others, and it touches, through some hidden similarity or minor characteristic, something deeply repressed in the unconscious, a deeply hidden wish, and opens up the floodgate through which that wish can be expressed in symbolic form. The human organism strives to reduce excitations but also to activate memories so as to recall and perhaps re-experience earlier pleasures. That is how wishes are born, and wishes turn, in the hands of the psychotic, to murder, in the hands of the artist, to art. In the unconscious, nothing ever dies, nothing is ever past or forgotten, everything is present simultaneously, past, present and future come together there and thus the unconscious is a form of eternal life, it is, in fact, eternity. The stage of a theatre is a three dimensional objective correlative to the psychological space of the unconscious, and on that stage, past, present and future, dream and experience, all come together. The stage is the most real place in the world, because it is the most like the unconscious world buried in each of us.

Proust believed that the job of the artist was to release the creative energy of past experience from the abyss of the unconscious. Caroline Spurgeon's image cluster studies of Shakespeare are fascinating maps of this strange process going on, maps of creation itself, of the sudden bursting out of unconscious material when touched off by the immediate needs of giving life and purpose to a character in a hackneyed story and charging it with that powerful eccentricity and sense of truth that makes Shakespeare an infinitely rich source of pleasure and knowledge while those literary sources from which he fashioned his plays remain historical curiosities. It was the deep and powerful ignition of Shakespeare's protean and near-bursting unconscious taking fire in the inferno of his soul that fashioned on a stage universes of incredible suggestiveness and resonance, more than one can fathom in a lifetime of seeing and reading. In the modern theatre, playwrights are not supposed to do this, plays are supposed to be written rationally, to move one dull step at a time, lest the audience, conceived by the collective theatre establishment to be monumentally stupid, lose track and grow frustrated. This is the tragedy of American theatre, that all too often it is a whorehouse theatre manufactured by the superficial for the benefit of the stupid.

10 (Dogma)

I don't write about women because I think I understand them, I write about them because they're important to me. I don't understand them any more than Freud did. In fact, I don't understand much of anything, and in the vast multitude of things I don't understand, I find myself writing again and again about those incomprehensible things I care about most. Sometimes writing about these things helps me to discover what they are, and often it helps me, if not to understand them any better, at least to map more clearly the geography of my miscomprehension. Writing is my own particular waltz. Perhaps on a given night I do it better than on other nights. It is quite possible for Freud to have been right about many things and dead wrong about many others. It is also possible for one to be dead wrong about something with no malicious intent. And it is certain that the best intentions can lead to very pernicious consequences. Perhaps this play is one of them. All of this is what art is about. Art is not dogma. Art is about how things make us feel. What we feel is a complex and ever-changing nightmare of horror and beauty. So is a play. If it all made perfectly good sense, it would be a fortune cookie. A theatre that worships simple-minded explanations is a theatre for cretins.

I like and respect Dora very much—she is the center of this play and the reason for its existence. It was my immediate attraction to her and fascination with the labyrinth of her complex dilemma, rather than any desire to attack or defend Freud or his theories, which made this play happen. And no doubt it was my own attraction to Dora which led me to be suspicious of Freud's hidden feelings for her. All symptoms, as Freud says, are overdetermined— each effect is a kind of melding of several causes. My attempt to understand Dora became a play about Freud's attempt to understand Dora, which in turn became a play about their attempts to understand each other. I have no idea which of them is right about Frau Klippstein. I don't think that's the point. When Dora dances at the end, it doesn't mean she's admitting Freud was right, or that she's proving he was wrong by managing to live a reasonably healthy life without having admitted to herself that his interpretation of her feelings for Frau Klippstein was correct. I don't think she knows for sure who is right, either. The point is not that she will ever know for certain. The point is that she dances.

11 (Truth)

There is something inexplicable at the heart of every play, some unanswered question deeply involved in its genesis, it corresponds to something in the playwright, some troubled or unfinished thing in the maker, a need which he cannot verbalize, some private ancient nightmare in his soul. The play that emerges is not the nightmare itself, cannot be, the nightmare is locked in his own flesh. What happens instead is that some external thing, a book, a chance remark, a girl seen in a certain light in bed on a certain morning, a myth, a fragment of history, a letter, a phrase of music—some chance event will unexpectedly echo in his soul, will connect to and embody in some way the deeper thing, the seed inside him which is the nightmare, but which has no voice, and the thing with no voice will begin to speak, and he will know, if he has chosen Shakespeare's difficult profession, that he must fashion the nightmare into words that can be translated in a theatre into flesh again, and so the nightmare passes from deep in the flesh of the maker through a little myth in his universe into a pattern that becomes other flesh—a play for actors to make alive on a stage in a theatre for other lost persons gathered together in a congregation. A play does not come from a rational place, it is not a rational animal, a play is a poem of flesh and blood that moves and bleeds. Art is about what cannot be expressed in rational discourse. It is not reducible to themes and formulas. It is about what is real but unspeakable, felt but ultimately unknowable except as symbol—living, ambiguous, protean.

Freud believed that he was charting territory in the human soul that poets and playwrights had already spoken of and fashioned into myth. His task, as he saw it, was to explore this territory not as a poet, but as a scientist and man of reason, like Theseus trying to map the labyrinth as he wandered in it. He wanted to find the truth, and to reduce the suffering of his tormented and unhappy patients. And he believed, as I understand him, that to do the one was, if not to accomplish the other, at least to come as close as one could get, in a universe built of constantly regenerating pain and loneliness. Ultimately, of course, what he did was create another mythology, a mythology of great, evolving complexity and some beauty, which we, as his intellectual children, now find ourselves living in.

But every created thing is distorted by time and chance and by the limitations of both the creator himself and of those disciples into whose hands the created thing must inevitably fall. It becomes an instrument for both good and evil, it liberates some and imprisons others, its truths are transformed by the inexorable clockworks of its fate into lies. And each creator is a human being, an imperfect, frail and dying thing, with human needs and fears which distort the quest and the creation. The investigator is always culpable. He is not outside the situation. His relationship with the patient *becomes* the situation. And the truth is a thing between them, they share it, see it differently, lose it, find it again together.

Dora's truth cannot be Freud's truth, and his truth cannot be hers. At the place where these truths touch there is something like a love story, love being what compels us to connect with others, and this inevitably fragile connection, not quite made, or made and then broken by time and chance, is the source of pain and art, is finally incomprehensible to us, and is the only truth which cannot be taken from us. Whatever truth we see, Freud's or Dora's or our own, if we are to continue to be sane, sanity in this case being whatever gives us the ability to continue, we accept the suffering, find if we can some compassion for those who make up the geography of our pain, take a deep breath, and, each in our own fashion and as best we can, we dance.

12 (Dreams of Flesh and Blood: a talk given on the stage of the McCarter Theatre on the campus of Princeton University, March 1, 1988.)

I'm going to talk to you for a bit about dreams and their relationship to flesh and blood, and about what I perceive to be the shared obsessions of three mythological figures who have at one time or another appeared in my plays— God, Shakespeare and Freud. You may object, perhaps, to my terminology. You may believe that only God qualifies as a mythological figure. Or, if you are a religious person and also happen to be a disciple of Delia Bacon or some other such loveable crackpot you might believe that God is not a mythological figure, but Shakespeare is. Freud, by the way, was in fact such a crackpot—he tended towards the elitist theory that Shakespeare was the Earl of Oxford or some other snotty member of the nobility, a theory based on the conviction that no boy from an obscure small town in the countryside with a somewhat slapdash education working in the professional theatre could possibly have written great works of dramatic literature. I take great exception to this form of Fascist snobbery, being myself coincidentally a boy from an obscure small town in the countryside with a somewhat slapdash education working in the professional theatre and attempting to create a serious body of dramatic literature. In fact, I am in actuality the fourth in this sequence of mythological figures, and probably the one I am really talking about, as much of what fascinates me about the other three is that they seem to me to have been engaged in the same activity that is my obsession, that is, in manufacturing little universes and watching them run.

First, let's talk about God, and then we can make our way down the old mythological ladder through Shakespeare and Freud down to my present position on one of the bottom rungs, next to the cow patties and discarded condoms and such. Some people, of course, would put Shakespeare somewhat ahead of God—I know this because when I wrote a play that was somewhat irreverent towards both God and Shakespeare, nobody complained much about the wisecracks about God, but several people were prepared to lynch me about Shakespeare, which seemed to me very odd, because I've spent most of my life with Shakespeare and consider him a pretty good friend, whereas many of the people who rushed indignantly to his defense seemed to have very little recent acquaintance with him, and tended to ascribe some of his obscenities to me and vice versa. What these people would think of my as yet unpublished dissertation on the symbolic importance of pissing images in Shakespeare and the King James Bible, I don't dare even think about. However. What was I saying? Oh, yes, God first, for old time's sake.

Now, God in the Old Testament is a notoriously cranky fellow, but I'm speaking here particularly of God in his early guise as Creator, in the first chapters of Genesis. God makes a world and peoples it with personages made more or less in his own image, and then watches in horror as it runs completely out of control—an experience that Shakespeare and I have had often in production, and which Freud may have felt when reading the works of his disciple Jung, say. I've often wondered what made God, the first mythological hero, decide to create the world. I presume from my own experience that it was probably loneliness. Whatever company good and bad angels might have been, the fact is, human beings are much more interesting, largely because of their immense capacity for screwing up grotesquely and then somehow recovering in time to create totally unexpected moments of beauty and joy. God's angels were either worshippers or devils, that is, they were political types—they were not, like him, creators. He was probably lonesome for some other creature touched with his own weakness, made in his image, so to speak, that is, with the capacity and urge to create. Of course, God screwed up, like all creators, because his creation had a mind of its own, and it took him, as writing often does, to unexpected places he probably did not want to go to, places of mixed tragedy and burlesque, laced with horror and great beauty.

Now, Shakespeare seems to me to have been possessed of this same restless urge to make universes that the God of Genesis apparently suffered from. Borges, the blind Argentine writer, paints in one of his little stories a Shakespeare who has no face, no identity, who must create constantly to give himself new masks and become the people he has invented, to populate his world, and I wonder if the God of Genesis in his great loneliness did not in fact begin creating in part precisely because he feared that he did not in fact exist. To have created something makes evidence, a residue of circumstance which at least implies indirectly that one existed once. If Borges and I are correct, then God and Shakespeare created for similar reasons— loneliness and a nagging fear that they did not exist. And God's later attempt, in the New Testament, to became an actor in his own badly screwed up play, in the form of

Christ, is paralleled by Shakespeare's and my own attempts to act. There was a time in the course of my jagged progress as a writer when I began to notice that my plays tended to fall into two general groups—Garden of Eden plays about creation and fall, and Passion plays about betrayal and crucifixion. Shakespeare and God and I experienced both—the actor goes out there naked and is crucified each night by the audience, and dies for their sins.

Now, the most persistent and powerful cluster of images and ideas in the plays of Shakespeare is for me not Caroline Spurgeon's famous slobbering, fawning dog and sweets clusters, although I am very fond of Miss Spurgeon's work. It is rather that recurring obsession of his with life as dream, dream as theatre, and theatre as life. In Shakespeare it seems that life, dream and theatre are all ultimately the same thing: all the world's a stage, and all the men and women merely players—When we are born we cry that we are come to this great stage of fools—life's but a walking shadow, a poor player, that struts and frets his hour upon the stage and then is heard no more—These, our actors, were all spirits and are melted into air, into thin air, and like the baseless fabric of this vision shall dissolve and like this insubstantial pageant faded, leave not a rack behind. We are such stuff as dreams are made on, and our little life is rounded with a sleep. Again and again in Shakespeare the world is a theatre and the theatre is a dream. Illusion is everything, and ripeness is all. The deepest moral in Shakespeare is to know your lines and play your action, right out to the end. And Freud, who saw both God and Shakespeare as mythological figures, who wrote *The Interpretation of Dreams* and *The Future of an Illusion,* who analyzed Hamlet and was fascinated by jokes and their relationship to the unconscious, insisted that he himself was only charting scientifically territory which artists like Shakespeare had explored before him.

Nietzsche spoke of theatre as the collective dream of the audience, a means of getting together to share unconscious experience, a way, perhaps, of hooking up together with Jung's collective unconscious, the bedrock that connects the islands of individual consciousness together far beneath the ocean of experience. What Freud seems to me to have done is to create a very powerful and complex mythology out of a life's body of work—the Garden in Genesis is God's dream, the theatre is Shakespeare's dream, and Freud dredges up his elaborate mythology out of his own dreams and those of his patients, sharing them and blending them together into a kind of synthesis that begins as neurosis, becomes science and then rapidly evolves like all science into art and therefore into mythology in which the creator Freud himself becomes, like God and Shakespeare before him, the most interesting and dominant character. Thus do religion, art and science all become one thing in the end— all that is lasting in religion and science becomes art, is absorbed into the collective dream of succeeding generations, becomes the story we tell over and over again about ourselves, like folktales, television, comic books, Bible stories, plays. Man is the creature that tells endless stories about himself, as in psychoanalysis, theatre, and the Bible. A ritual like a church service, a play, or a session with your analyst is the objective correlative of a mythologizing process that is what we are, those who create, those who make little universes and watch them run.

One of the more horrible things about creation, of course, is that the beautiful and complex mythologies we generate tend to inevitably fall into the hands of persons themselves hostile to creation, and thus we see God's universe becoming organized religion and turning into a machine for murdering people with dogma, we see Shakespeare's plays turned into cultural icons of rigor mortis used to oppress and persecute generations of innocent school children, and we see Freud's ideas used to oppress, steal, enslave, control. Thus does all creation inevitably turn into destruction. Eros becomes Thanatos. God wonders if he should not destroy what he has made. Prospero buries his magic book and Shakespeare goes home to Stratford. Freud is forced into exile and dies on the brink of a hideous war. The young Nazi soldiers who come to Freud's house in Vienna, take his daughter Anna away for hours of questioning, and are shamed momentarily by his wife's offer of tea and cookies, these are the messengers of the inevitable destruction of all created things. God's book ends with Armageddon, Shakespeare's with the end of magic and the abandonment of the island-theatre dream, and Freud's life ends in Shakespeare's London, under fire, in terrible pain, his world destroyed, Thanatos triumphant. All created things are mortal, all creation ends in destruction, ripeness is all, we must play our action while we can, and the theatre is for me the ripest place in the universe.

Only in the theatre are dreams made flesh and blood. A novel is in the head, and so is a movie—and both are in a sense disembodied and dreamlike by nature. But in the theatre the dream is flesh and blood, the people are in the same room with you, you can see them sweat, watch them stumble, smell the perfume on the ladies—it is the proximity of actual flesh and blood that makes theatre a fundamentally different and more primary dream-experience than the novel or the motion picture can be. The fact of the actor's mortality, of his potential for error, the immediacy of the situation and the necessity of recreating all over again the dream each night are unique to the theatre. Theatre is very difficult. The dream resists. One forgets one's lines. The lights go out, the prop gun does not fire, one trips on the rug, that person with the severe coughing disorder who seems to come to all my plays is making horrible noises in the audience and this obscures a line which must then be repeated or forever lost—it is this constant interplay between the attention of the audience and the struggle of the actors to give flesh to the play which makes theatre such an intense and unique experience. And it is precisely what can and usually does go wrong in a given performance that convinces us of the unique and precious danger involved in making theatre happen. I cannot feel close to theatre which gets away from flesh and blood. The further away from the actors you get, the less you are actually experiencing theatre itself. It is the proximity of the actor that makes the theatre live. A play is a poem of flesh and blood that moves. A play is a work of literature meant to be read, then translated into flesh and blood, and thus to enter into the minds of the assembled congregation, and thus does dream become written artifact become flesh and blood become dream again.

Theatre is how we share dreams, but it is this ritual passage through flesh and blood that makes the dream so vivid. A myth is an archetypal story, the distillation of something that happens again and again in human experience, shared experience, part of the cultural heritage that mirrors the genetic heritage inside us. A ritual is the flesh and blood enactment of a myth. Theatre is the ritual which makes flesh and blood of the archetypal myth the playwright has written down. The performance is the body and the play (the thing written down) is the soul—the soul moves from body to body as in reincarnation, constantly being reborn in the flesh of different actors in different productions through the centuries.

As we follow Freud through the twisted labyrinth of mysteries that make up Dora's world, we become, like him, increasingly co-opted by them, pulled in until Freud has himself become one of them, like God and Shakespeare before him. It is not an accident that certain forms of medieval drama arising out of church services should have been called mystery plays. Every play is a mystery. In order to solve Dora's mystery, Freud evolves a set of theories—he creates an explanation, makes an interpretation in his own image, as Dora has made one in hers, and we, in turn, watching these people move in and out of each other's lives, must create our own universe of meaning as we watch. Who is telling the truth? When the creator God-Shakespeare-Freud gets pulled so deeply into his own creation that he becomes a character in it, can we trust him? Should we be able to trust an analyst, a playwright, a God with a truth, or must we find it again and again for ourselves? The mystery of the play becomes a mirror. As all science eventually turns into mythology, and all history eventually becomes literature or else sinks into oblivion, so all historical figures eventually become mythological figures as we move further and further away from them in time. Freud and Dora become God and Eve, Shakespeare and the Dark Lady, or us and the person we love. We watch them reincarnated as flesh and blood and we become them, devour them, take them into ourselves in that profound act of communion that is theatre.

One writes a play and then one lives it. One sees a play and one becomes it. The greatest mystery is that we are made of flesh and blood and yet we also feel that we are something else. In performance the union of spirit with flesh and blood seems to happen in such a way that we communally carry on our dream investigation to wherever it may lead us—to Dora's truth or Freud's truth, or to some truth in between. In Indian mythology the world is seen as a great dance, and this play is like a dance, the dance being our willingness to enter into some active relationship with the eternal mystery of flesh and blood. In most plays, things tend to lope along in single file—the maid talks to the butler, there's some boring exposition while you get settled in your seats, people you don't care about talk about people you don't know and haven't seen yet. Well, I don't like that, so in this play you get to see most of the people who get talked about right away, while they're being talked about, because they're already there— everybody who matters is there, all of the time, so we're relieved of all that tedious business of people knocking on doors and thinking up excuses to leave the room so some other boring scene can happen. Also, I hate sitting in the dark between scenes while people dressed in black clunk around on the stage rearranging the furniture, so in this play all the people have to do to be somewhere else is just to turn around and look at somebody who's in a different place, and, bingo, we're there. It's very easy. If theatre is the place where all times and places co-exist, then why can't we see them all at the same time? Some would characterize this as a departure from realism, but from my point of view, what generally passes for realism in the theatre is not very real. I don't think the maid and the butler really would talk like that—As you know, twelve years ago when the young master went away to sea, he vowed to return and marry Miss Susie—well, come on, if the guy already knows this, then why the hell is she telling him? Because it's a play, of course, and a pretty wretched one at that.

Let me describe the way experience feels to me. I'm walking down the street in the morning, talking to a dog, say, who's walking along beside me—maybe that big, fat tan dog who's always eating out of garbage cans just outside the theatre—and while I'm talking to this dog, I'm reminded of a lady math teacher I had in grade school whom this dog very much resembles, and I'm also thinking about the old guy who's going to interview me for the newspaper and with a part of my mind I'm also imagining what a certain movie actress must look like naked. Now, all of this is happening pretty much at the same time, see—so there's a sense in which, in my experience, the dog, the math teacher, the interviewer and the naked movie star are all present at the same time, and this is what reality is like to me—the past, the present, the future and fantasy are all interpenetrating at every moment. And since the stage is that place where all times and places co-exist, focus, come together in a communal dream, it's the perfect place, in some ways the only place, in which I can physically embody what this multi-dimensional experience of reality really feels like. Simultaneous existence is much more difficult to suggest in linear forms like the novel and the motion picture. So the stage is, paradoxically, a very real place, on which very real dreams are fashioned. And in this play you see people relating across time and space in the same way they do every day, and I suspect nearly every second, of your experience.

There is one last thing. I want to share with you what it feels like to be a playwright. Actors have dreams, essentially the same dream, talk to an actor and you will hear a version of this dream: you're on stage and don't know your lines, you've got to go on and you can't remember what the play is, you can't find the theatre and it's one minute to curtain, you're onstage and cannot hear or understand what the other actors are saying, you're backstage and hear your cue and find yourself running through gelatin trying to get to the stage—it's all really the same dream. Well, I want to share with you a playwright's dream, one that I had early in my career, and to this day the most vivid dream I've ever had: I'm in a theatre. Backstage. Loud music. The end of a show. A chorus line of overweight dancers are high-kicking the finale. There are old men backstage, playing cards. The show ends. The music finishes. And there is absolute silence. The old men look up. Stillness. Nothing. One old man gets up, puts on his coat and hat, and leaves—he is the producer. A little old bald stage manager leads me to the curtain, and I go and look out into the audience. All the seats are filled, but with stiff, headless bodies dressed in suits and evening gowns. There are rows and rows of headless bodies in all the seats in the theatre. Young people are putting the stiff, headless bodies on stretchers and taking them away, pinning a small, white piece of paper over the heart of each, a bloodstain on each paper. I stand alone on the stage and I hear somebody screaming. Then I realize, the person screaming is in my head. I have become trapped forever in a dream of flesh and blood.

13 (Music)

I have keyed the measure numbers in the text to the sheet music version printed in *Memories of Johann Strauss, 12 Most Famous Waltzes for Piano Solo*, published by Edward B. Marks Music Corporation. The recorded versions of the waltzes I recommend are *The Blue Danube: A Johann Strauss Festival*, with the Philadelphia Orchestra Conducted by Eugene Ormandy (Columbia Masterworks MS 6217), for the "Emperor Waltz" especially, but also for a good, strong "Blue Danube" and a rich "Vienna Blood" (which is sometimes translated incorrectly on purpose as "Vienna Life" on some albums). For "Tales from the Vienna Woods" I strongly suggest the version on *Strauss, The Immortal Waltzes: Tales of the Vienna Woods, Voices of Spring and Others*, Vienna Peoples Opera Orchestra, Anton Paulik, Conductor, Summit (SUM 5008)—CMS Records, 226 Washington Street, Mount Vernon, NY 10553. This version uses a zither instead of violins on the delicate section that forms the background for the second act entrance and the wood nymph fantasy, the zither being much eerier and more appropriate for our purposes than the tamer violins of the Ormandy version. You may also prefer the version of "Vienna Blood" in this album, which is not as rich as the Ormandy but eerier for the nightmare scenes. The music for the dream and calliope (or orchestron) sequences should be a bit distorted and chilling, but should not under any circumstances have a sterile, electronic quality. An old church organ or silent movie organ is best. Water, woods and blood. The waltz is magic, sex, flesh and blood, never sterile or mechanical. It is the basic rhythm of life.

SWEET IS THE MAIDEN

OH SWEET IS THE MAI-DEN AND SWEET IS THE HILL U-PON WHICH I LAY DOWN AND LOVE DID FUL-FILL - OH SWEET IS THE RI-VER THAT FLOWS IN ITS BED, THE RI-VER WHERE MY LOVE'S SWEET SOUL SWIFT-LY SPED AND SWEET IS THE WILD WOOD, HOME OF THE TALL TREE, THE WILD WOOD WILL STAND STRONG AND BRING MY LOVE TO ME - THE WILD WOOD WILL STAND STRONG, HOME OF THE TALL TREE AND THE RI-VER WILL CA-A-RY MY TRUE LOVE HOME TO MEE MY TRUE LOVE HOME TO MEEE MY TRUE LOVE HOME TOOOO MEEEE

Other Publications for Your Interest

CINDERELLA WALTZ
(ALL GROUPS—COMEDY)
By DON NIGRO

4 men, 5 women—1 set

Rosey Snow is trapped in a fairy tale world that is by turns funny and a little frightening, with her stepsisters Goneril and Regan, her demented stepmother, her lecherous father, a bewildered Prince, a fairy godmother who sings salty old sailor songs, a troll and a possibly homicidal village idiot. A play which investigates the archetypal origins of the world's most popular fairy tale and the tension between the more familiar and charming Perrault version and the darker, more ancient and disturbing tale recorded by the brothers Grimm. Grotesque farce and romantic fantasy blend in a fairy tale for adults.

(#5208)

ROBIN HOOD
(LITTLE THEATRE—COMEDY)
By DON NIGRO

14 men, 8 women—(more if desired.) Unit set.

In a land where the rich get richer, the poor are starving, and Prince John wants to cut down Sherwood Forest to put up an arms manufactory, a slaughterhouse and a tennis court for the well to do, this bawdy epic unites elements of wild farce and ancient popular mythologies with an environmentalist assault on the arrogance of wealth and power in the face of poverty and hunger. Amid feeble and insane jesters, a demonic snake oil salesman, a corrupt and lascivious court, a singer of eerie ballads, a gluttonous lusty friar and a world of vivid and grotesque characters out of a Brueghel painting, Maid Marian loses her clothes and her illusions among the poor and Robin tries to avoid murder and elude the Dark Monk of the Wood who is Death and also perhaps something more.

(#20075)

Other Publications for Your Interest

THE CURATE SHAKESPEARE AS YOU LIKE IT
(LITTLE THEATRE—COMEDY)
By DON NIGRO

4 men, 3 women—Bare stage

This extremely unusual and original piece is subtitled: "The record of one company's attempt to perform the play by William Shakespeare". When the very prolific Mr. Nigro was asked by a professional theatre company to adapt *As You Like It* so that it could be performed by a company of seven he, of course, came up with a completely original play about a rag-tag group of players comprised of only seven actors led by a dotty old curate who nonetheless must present Shakespeare's play; and the dramatic interest, as well as the comedy, is in their hilarious attempts to impersonate all of Shakespeare's multitude of characters. The play has had numerous productions nationwide, all of which have come about through word of mouth. We are very pleased to make this "underground comic classic" widely available to theatre groups who like their comedy wide open and theatrical. (#5742)

SEASCAPE WITH SHARKS AND DANCER
(LITTLE THEATRE—DRAMA)
By DON NIGRO

1 man, 1 woman—Interior

This is a fine new play by an author of great talent and promise. We are very glad to be introducing Mr. Nigro's work to a wide audience with *Seascape With Sharks and Dancer*, which comes directly from a sold-out, critically acclaimed production at the world-famous Oregon Shakespeare Festival. The play is set in a beach bungalow. The young man who lives there has pulled a lost young woman from the ocean. Soon, she finds herself trapped in his life and torn between her need to come to rest somewhere and her certainty that all human relationships turn eventually into nightmares. The struggle between his tolerant and gently ironic approach to life and her strategy of suspicion and attack becomes a kind of war about love and creation which neither can afford to lose. In other words, this is quite an offbeat, wonderful love story. We would like to point out that the play also contains a wealth of excellent **monologue** and **scene material.** (#21060)